KU-157-727

Pupil Welfare and Counselling: An Approach to Personal and Social Education across the Curriculum

David Galloway

GWENT COLLEGE OF HIGHER EDUCATION
LIBRARY

LONGMAN
London and New York

203261

Longman Group UK Limited,
Longman House, Burnt Mill, Harlow,
Essex CM20 2JE, England
and Associated Companies throughout the world.

*Published in the United States of America
by Longman Inc., New York*

© Longman Group UK Limited 1990

All rights reserved; no part of this publication may be
reproduced, stored in a retrieval system, or transmitted in
any form or by any means, electronic, mechanical,
photocopying, recording, or otherwise, without the prior
written permission of the Publishers.

First published 1990

British Library Cataloguing in Publication Data
Galloway, David M. (David Malcolm), 1942–
  Pupil welfare and counselling: An approach to Personal
  and Social Education across the Curriculum – (The
  effective teacher series)
  1. Great Britain. Secondary schools. Students.
  Counselling
  I. Title   II. Series
  373.14,0941

ISBN 0-582-00330-X

Library of Congress Cataloging in Publication Data
Galloway, David, 1942–
  Pupil welfare and counselling: An approach to Personal
  and Social Education across the Curriculum / by David
  Galloway.
     p.   cm. – (The effective teacher series)
  Bibliography: p.
  Includes index.
  ISBN 0-582-00330-X : £5.95 (est.)
  1. Teacher-student relationships. 2. Personnel service
  in education.   3. Teaching.   I. Title.   II. Series.
    LB1033.G283   1990   89-2602
    371.1'023–dc20   CIP

Produced by Longman Group (FE) Limited
Printed in Hong Kong

CONTENTS

EDITOR'S PREFACE

This new series was inspired by my book on the practice of teaching, (*Effective Teaching: a practical guide to improving your teaching*. Longman 1982) written for teacher training students as well as for in-service teachers wishing to improve their teaching skills. The books in this series have been written with the same readership in mind. However, the busy classroom teacher will also find that the books serve their needs as changes in the nature and pattern of education make the retraining of experienced teachers more essential than in the past.

The rationale behind the series is that professional courses for teachers require the coverage of a wide variety of subjects in a relatively short time. So the aim of the series is the production of 'easy to read', practical guides to provide the necessary subject background, supported by references to encourage and guide further reading together with questions and/or exercises devised to assist application and evaluation.

As specialists in their selected fields, the authors have been chosen for their ability to relate their subjects closely to the needs of teachers and to stimulate discussion of contemporary issues in education.

The series covers subjects ranging from *The Theory of Education* to *The Teaching of Mathematics* and from *The Psychology of Learning* to *Health Education*. It will look at aspects of education as diverse as *Education and Cultural Diversity* and *Assessment in Education*, *The Effective Teaching of English* and *The History of Education*. Although some titles such as *The Administration of Education* are specific to England and Wales, the majority of titles, such as *Comparative Education, The Effective Teaching of Modern Languages*, *The Use of Computers in Teaching* and *Pupil Welfare and Counselling* will be international in scope.

In a period when education is a subject of general debate and is operating against a background of major change, there is little doubt that the books, although of primary interest to teachers, will also find a wider readership.

Elizabeth Perrott

AUTHOR'S PREFACE

Aims, scope and structure of the book

This book is an introduction to pupil welfare, personal and social education, and counselling. My aim has been to identify the common ground between welfare and counselling and the 'core' elements of the teacher's classroom work. I have also tried to show how these core elements inevitably exert an important influence on pupils' personal and social development. The book shows how the psychology, sociology and philosophy of education can help to clarify welfare and counselling issues which from time to time affect the education of all pupils. I hope that the book will help students and more experienced teachers: (i) to incorporate and apply in their day-to-day work an understanding of welfare issues in the broadest sense; (ii) to develop basic counselling skills in working with children, parents, and their own colleagues; (iii) to acquire an understanding of the multiple ways in which they are likely to influence their pupils' personal and social development.

These aims require knowledge and understanding of the scope and limits to the teacher's responsibility (Chapter 2); curriculum and organisational implications of welfare, counselling, and personal and social education (Chapters 3 and 4); skills needed in talking about personally sensitive issues with groups of children and with individuals (Chapters 5 and 6); communication with parents (Chapter 7); effective use of the support services (Chapter 8); and effective work with colleagues (Chapter 9).

Using the book

The book is designed for use by groups of teachers on INSET courses and by tutorial or seminar groups of students on B. Ed. and PGCE courses. My hope is that it will encourage people to reflect on their own experience and thereby stimulate constructively critical discussion. Questions and exercises are provided at the end of each chapter. These are intended for guidance only and do not aim to address all the issues raised in the chapter. If discussion provoked by the book helps teachers to review and evaluate provision for pupils' welfare in their own schools I will feel that it has achieved its purpose. If it helps them to plan and introduce changes that improve the quality of pupil care, and of personal and social education in their schools I shall be delighted.

David Galloway
January 1989

ACKNOWLEDGEMENTS

We are grateful to the following for permission to reproduce copyright material; the author, Raymond Garlick for his poem 'Thug' in *Collected Poems 1946–1986* (pub Gwasg Gomer, 1987); Harmony Music Ltd & Cherry Lane Music Publishing Co, Inc for the song 'What did you learn in School today?' by Tom Paxton © 1966 words & music by Tom Paxton, Cherry Lane Music Co, Inc, assigned to Harmony Music Ltd, © Copyright 1962, 1964 Cherry Lane Music Publishing Co, Inc, International copyright secured, all rights reserved.

ABBREVIATIONS

DES	Department of Education and Science
DHSS	Department of Health and Social Security
EWO	Educational Welfare Officer
GCSE	General Certificate of Secondary Education
HMI	Her Majesty's Inspector of Schools
ILEA	Inner London Education Authority
INSET	In Service Training
LEA	Local Education Authority
MSC	Manpower Services Commission
NSPCC	National Society for the Prevention of Cruelty to Children
PGCE	Post Graduate Certificate of Education
PSE	Personal and Social Education

DISCLAIMERS

The views expressed in this book are the author's own and should not be taken to reflect those of individuals or institutions who co-operated with any of the inquiries referred to in the book. When presenting case histories, and when quoting teachers or pupils verbatim I have changed names, abbreviations of names, nicknames and other identifying characteristics.

CHAPTER 1

Teachers, not welfare workers?

Introduction

Teachers in Britain have traditionally prided themselves on their concern for the 'whole child'. This has attracted international attention as a central feature of primary schools following publication of the Plowden Report (DES, 1967), and is also reflected in the pastoral care networks of secondary schools. It contrasts with the narrow curricular focus of some countries in Europe. French teachers, for example, are reported as being amazed by the range of tasks which their English counterparts take for granted (e.g. Mille, 1987). Most teachers in Britain feel that they do, and should, accept some degree of responsibility for their pupils' overall welfare, even though 'welfare problems' are not infrequently a source of frustration and stress. They may disagree on the scope of their own responsibility vis-à-vis that of parents and the various education and social work support services, but few would wish to insist that their responsibilities stopped with teaching a predetermined syllabus without reference to the wider needs of particular individuals in their care.

Yet behind the professional, and legal, consensus, that teachers are *in loco parentis*, and hence have duties that go beyond a strict interpretation of the curriculum, considerable tensions are evident. Studies of pastoral care in secondary schools reveal a preoccupation with discipline and with organisation and routine (e.g. Best *et al*, 1980). Similar tensions are evident in primary schools (e.g. David and Charlton, 1987; Lang, 1988). Further, there is clear evidence that the partnership with parents, so often extolled in school prospectuses, is at best an unequal one. Teachers complain that the parents they most need to see are those who are least likely to visit the school. For their part these parents associate visits to school with criticisms from teachers for their children's failures.

What is actually meant by concern for the whole child remains tantalisingly unclear. It presumably includes a commitment to pupils' personal and social development. Yet in spite of a burgeoning literature, both the nature and scope of personal and social education remain controversial. The links between this and the other aspects of pupils' life and work at school are seldom clear. The same is true of the links between personal and social education and the welfare activities for which teachers claim or accept responsibility.

Accepting responsibility for pupils' welfare could imply that teachers have made a professional judgement about the nature of teaching. It could also imply that the government and/or employing LEAs have made a decision about the scope of teachers' duties. In a curious way, both are true. At the height of their industrial action in 1985-1987, some teachers' associations withdrew co-operation in all activities that fell outside their existing contracts. As well as extra-curricular functions, including sport, drama and music, and curriculum planning exercises, this also affected welfare-related tasks, for example parents' evenings. At no time, though, was it suggested that these were peripheral to the basic nature of the job.

Yet in spite of teachers' acceptance of responsibility for pupil welfare, or possibly because of it, the government has taken an increasingly directive interest in pupil welfare. Following the industrial action it imposed conditions of service which, for the first time, explicitly required teachers to communicate and consult with parents and outside bodies, take part in meetings about pastoral arrangements and promote 'the general progress and well-being of individual pupils and of any class or group of pupils' assigned to them (DES, 1988a, p.23). In addition, the Education Acts of 1980, 1986 and 1988 radically altered the previous balance of power between the DES, LEAs, teachers and parents. Briefly, the consistent and cumulative effect has been to shift power from LEAs and teachers to central government, governors and parents. This will have enormous implications both for the relationships which teachers develop with their pupils' parents and for the way they conceptualise and plan personal and social education. Both are related to welfare. It is time, therefore, to define welfare and related terms.

Terminology

Pupil Welfare

Adapting the shorter Oxford Dictionary, pupil welfare activities may be defined as those which contribute to pupils' happiness or well-being. This seems consistent with the focus on 'general progress and well-being' in the Teachers' Conditions of Services document (DES, 1988a). It does, however, raise three important tissues.

1. Pupils' happiness or well-being at school is obviously affected by their sense of progress and achievement in the curriculum.

Are we, then, to assume that everything that happens in school, including all aspects of the curriculum are intrinsically related to pupil welfare? This may well be true, but does not really help to explain exactly what we are talking about. How teachers think about welfare, and about the related area of personal and social education has implications both for curriculum content and for teaching methods. Saying this, though, does not imply lack of recognition for activities which take place outside the official, or national curriculum.

2. Pupils' well-being at school is affected by factors outside the school. At the simplest level, there is no controversy about the relationship between children's educational attainments and their parents' occupation: children with professional parents tend to leave both primary and secondary school with higher educational attainments than children with parents in manual occupations. The reasons are certainly controversial, as is the extent of the school's influence, but the underlying tendency is not in dispute. Within many staff-rooms children's learning or behaviour difficulties are attributed to factors in their home backgrounds. Sometimes the explanation is manifestly simplistic. The term 'broken home', for example, reveals nothing about the reasons for the parents' separation, and implicitly overlooks the possibility that a child may have a stronger and more secure relationship with both parents after they have separated than before. Yet although the relationship between children's performance at school and the pressures they experience outside school, either at home or in the neighbourhood, is seldom straightforward, the fact that *some* relationship frequently exists is not controversial.

   This raises an important question about the limits to a school's responsibility for pupil welfare. The obvious answer is that teachers are concerned about factors *out* of school only in so far as they affect pupils' personal, social or educational welfare *at* school. This solution usually provides an adequate guideline, but as always there are exceptions. If teachers suspect that a child is being physically or sexually abused they are expected to inform the appropriate authorites (see Chapter 8) even if there is no obvious evidence that the pupil's progress or adjustment at school is being affected. Similarly, suspicion of involvement in serious criminal activity requires teachers to take action. A more difficult question arises when teachers feel that pupils' educational welfare requires removal from homes they regard as unsuitable, while colleagues in other services insist that their overall welfare in the long-term would be harmed by removal. This brings us to the third issue arising from our definition of welfare.

3. Happiness and well-being are value-laden concepts which

depend on the priorities or ideology, of the person who holds them. Within every school, teachers will vary in how they define their priorities and in their underlying assumptions about children and about the aims of education. At national level, the Conservative government of the 1980's, explicitly sought to encourage competition within and between schools. Some LEAs sought, just as explicitly, to discourage a competitive ethos. Similar differences in philosophy are found within schools. Inevitably, they affect the way teachers think about the welfare aspects of their job. Nowhere is this more evident than in counselling interviews.

Counselling

In counselling, one individual, the counsellor, works with another, the client, to clarify the nature of some problem experienced or presented by the client, and to explore possible solutions. Counselling can also take place in a group but the essential characteristics remain, namely that it is problem-oriented, and that it involves the interrelated stages of clarifying the nature of the problem and exploring possible solutions.

An essential issue in our definition of counselling is that many, perhaps a majority, of interviews in school are held at the request of teachers, not of pupils or their parents. This raises ethical and practical questions to which we shall return in chapter six. Briefly, though, interviews which in the broadest sense have a problem-solving orientation are regarded here as counselling interviews.

This does not, of course, mean that all interviews with teachers and pupils or their parents are counselling interviews. Some interviews with pupils have an essentially disciplinary function. They may require the teacher to exercise counselling skills, for example in ensuring that the child understands the point of the interview, but they are not counselling sessions. Similarly, some meetings with parents have the limited aim of passing on information or seeking agreement to a particular predetermined course of action, such as referral to the school doctor. Here, too, the teacher may need to use counselling skills, for example in overcoming hostility or suspicion, but these are not primarily counselling interviews.

There are, however, numerous occasions when every teacher interviews pupils and parents in order to clarify the nature of a problem and to consider possible courses of action. We will consider two common scenarios:

1. Ahmed's form tutor receives a complaint that he has failed to produce every English homework for the last six weeks. Other

teachers have not complained about his failure to complete their homework, but the form tutor suspects they may be taking the line of least resistance. He makes the following list of possible reasons: laziness; difficulty in coping with English as a second language; dislikes the English teacher; feels that his future is mapped out (Ahmed will work in his father's shop on leaving school), and regards English homework as a waste of time; conditions in the home unsuitable; lack of time for homework due to employment out of school hours; disaffection from school, associated with being on the fringe of a group of anti-authority teenagers; anxiety about the health of his mother who is known to have been in hospital on several occasions.

The form tutor's list is certainly not exhaustive. It does, however, give him a number of possibilities to consider when talking with Ahmed. It also indicates how an apparently straightforward problem may have complex origins.

2. The parents of ten-year-old Pauline ask to see her class teacher about her work. When they meet, the class teacher finds that Pauline's parents seem more concerned about her behaviour at home than her progress at school. The class teacher has received minor complaints about Pauline's behaviour from the dinner ladies, but none that would have justified contacting her parents.

Here, the pupil's parents indicate that they have worries which the school does not necessarily share. The class teacher is not a counsellor, social worker or psychologist. It is not her responsibility to help Pauline's parents with what may be a problem in their relationship with their daughter. On the other hand, the parents of a pupil have asked to see her. Hence, she does have a responsibility to clarify the nature of their problem in order to reach an informed decision on whether to discuss the possibility of the parents contacting one of the educational or social work support services.

All teachers will encounter situations like these. When handled sensitively they strengthen the pupil's or the parents' confidence in the school, and thereby facilitate the pupil's progress in the classroom. Unfortunately the reverse is also true. In addition, children will turn to teachers they trust with sensitive personal problems, such as the effect of family disputes, physical or sexual abuse, pregnancy and drug-taking.

How teachers handle situations in which children or parents raise personal problems with them must inevitably depend partly on their skill in handling personal interviews. The most effective primary class teachers may feel out of their depth when confronted with the distress and anger of a pupil whose parents have just separated. The most effective secondary subject teachers may feel out of their depth when talking to a 14-year-old who suspects she is pregnant.

Yet as well as their own professional skills, two further factors will influence teachers' responses. First, each person's current beliefs and values have developed from their previous experiences. Hence, a teacher's response to a particular incident may be coloured by his or her previous experiences. Second, any counselling that takes place *in* a school will be affected by the aims and ethos *of* the school. In other words, teachers cannot counsel pupils without some idea of the personal attributes which they as individuals or the school as an institution are aiming to encourage.

In passing it is worth mentioning that counselling is seldom, if ever, value-free. A counsellor may feel satisfied, if as a result of counselling, a pupil who has been experimenting with drugs reaches a decision to stop taking them. Few counsellors will feel satisfied if the same pupil, while abstaining himself, decides to use his leadership qualities to encourage addiction in fellow pupils, thereby earning, incidentally, considerably more than the headteacher, let alone the counsellor. Granted, then, that counselling is not value-free, it will be influenced by the values of the teacher concerned and/or of the school as a social institution. This takes us to personal and social education.

Personal and social education

For present purposes we define this simply as all learning experiences which give pupils a developing sense of their own abilities and of their rights and responsibilities as contributing members of the school and of the wider community in which they live. We shall consider in more detail later what may be implied by a 'developing' sense of their own abilities and of their rights and responsibilities (see Chapter 2). Here I wish only to emphasise that personal development is shaped by social experiences. Consequently, the 'personal' and 'social' elements of personal and social education are inextricably interrelated.

Successful teaching involves working with groups. If individual children's needs are met in mainstream primary and secondary classrooms, they are met through group activities. This is as true of all subjects in the national curriculum as of any personal and social education programmes. While acknowledging the central role of group activities, though, we should recognise that the personal, social and educational well-being of individual pupils will be affected, for better or worse, by a wide variety of additional factors over which teachers have some control.

Links between teaching, pupil welfare and counselling

Recognition that the quality of teaching contributes to pupils' overall welfare at school should not blind us to other even more basic influences. It is easy to recognise that some children's development may be adversely affected by their home circumstances, but more difficult to see how schools may also fail to recognise the basic need for physical security. Two vignettes illustrate this:

1. Jenny frequently had a runny nose. In the infants school a box of tissues was an indispensable part of her teacher's classroom equipment. She was described as being 'in a world of her own' and had a reputation for not listening to instructions. She had to be told everything twice. When she was nine her mother took her to the doctor because she was unusually 'chesty'. The doctor confirmed that she had an infection, but also diagnosed catarrhal deafness, often known as 'glue ear', associated with colds, minor infections and hay fever. There were times when she had no hearing loss. Yet her tendency to 'switch off' rather than concentrate in order to hear what the teacher said, continued even when she was physically fit. Since she started school her education had been affected by her hearing loss. By the time it was diagnosed, secondary problems of loss of motivation had developed.
2. The third and fourth year classes in a senior school were based in terrapins in the school playground and had a long-standing reputation for being hard to teach. When they moved classrooms teachers noticed after a few weeks that they had become much easier. Three years earlier a teacher had complained about the noise and flicker from the ancient striplights. The head had forwarded the complaint to County Hall but nothing had been done and the head had not persisted.

Maslow (1970) argued that people have a hierarchy of needs from the basic needs for food and drink to 'self-actualisation', or the sense of self-fulfilment that comes from achieving one's full potential. This hierarchy is summarised in Table 1.1. Maslow argued that people are only motivated to achieve higher level needs when lower level needs have been met. In fact this is not always the case. People frequently do not progress up the hierarchy in an orderly way. For example, some people may neglect lower-order needs in order to meet an intellectual challenge. Nevertheless, the two examples given above do illustrate how failure to meet lower-order needs may affect pupils' progress, resulting in frustration for pupil and teacher alike. No amount of curriculum development or attention to teaching methods would have made much difference. If we consider the fourth need on Marlow's hierarchy, self-esteem, the inter-relationship between teaching and welfare becomes even more evident.

Table 1.1 *Summary of Maslow's Hierarchy of Needs*

Highest Level	'self-actualisation'; the sense of self-fulfilment that comes from achieving one's full potential.
	Aesthetic appreciation
	Intellectual challenge and achievement
	Self-esteem: the need for approval and recognition
	Sense of belonging/membership of family, class, peer group
	Safety: the need to feel physically and psychologically secure
Lowest Level	Survival: basic needs for food, drink etc.

Adapted from: A. H. Maslow (1970)

Accepting a commitment to pupils' personal, social and educational welfare will lead us to reject the obvious explanations for low self-esteem such as a physical disability or low educational attainments, or at least to look beyond them. How pupils with minor physical impairments see themselves will depend to a large extent on how far the school's hidden curriculum accepts and respects individual differences. (We return to the hidden curriculum in Chapter 2.) Derogatory nicknames such as 'four eyes', or 'lippy' for a pupil with a speech defect, can have an all-pervading effect on a child's life at school. Similarly, if the school's hidden curriculum equates high status with academic success, so that pupils with special needs attract labels throughout the school such as 'divvies', it may be the label at least as much as the low attainment which negatively affects a pupil's motivation.

Even when a child is under pressure due to family circumstances, much will depend on how the school interprets the situation. Peter, for example, entered secondary school with a reputation from his primary school for bad behaviour and poor concentration. He quickly lived down to this reputation. Numerous minor incidents were reported to his form tutor and head of year. When they reviewed Peter's progress towards the end of his first term, they realised that almost all complaints related to incidents in the morning. Further investigation revealed that he had often had nothing to eat since his tea on arrival home at 4.30 pm the previous day. 'If your blood-sugar level was as low as that you wouldn't be able to concentrate either', the school nurse told the head of year.

Peter's case could be seen as just another insoluble social problem. In the event, a thoughtful form tutor made arrangements for Peter to collect, on arrival at school in the morning, a packet of crisps which he had purchased the previous day. It reflected well on the form tutor that she was able to discuss the problem with Peter and enlist his co-operation without attracting negative comment from other pupils.

The point is simply that effective teaching requires an undertanding of the differing needs and motivations of individual pupils. Our concern about individuals, however, should not obscure the more elementary point that these individuals are members of a class and of a school. As such, they will influence and be influenced by the ethos, or social climate of the class and of the school. Thus, while both personal and social education and pupil welfare start with an analysis of individual needs, and while teachers require knowledge of educational and social work support services which can help in meeting these needs, they are integrally linked with much broader questions about the curriculum and about school and classroom climate.

Conclusions

The period 1980–1988 witnessed four major Education Acts culminating in the 1988 Education Reform Act. After seeing their negotiating rights removed, teachers had to cope with the rapid introduction of a new public examination system in the General Certificate of Secondary Education, followed by the national curriculum, its associated attainment targets and testing programme, the possibility of schools opting out of local authority control if the parents and/or governors decided to seek grant-maintained status, and local financial management. Given this climate of constant change, teachers might be forgiven for thinking that welfare, counselling, and personal and social education would be submerged by the pressure of other demands. For two reasons, this view may be unduly pessimistic.

First, effective teaching implies recognition of the needs of individual pupils, with the ability to match the task to the pupil's ability (Bennett *et al*, 1984). The introduction of a national curriculum and associated attainment targets will not change this. Indeed, it may even lead to increased attention to pupils' welfare needs. The national curriculum will remove from teachers much of the pressure to determine curriculum content. It may thereby enable them to spend more time planning and evaluating the teaching process. In addition, the increase in parents' freedom to select their child's school will result in greater competition for pupils between schools. Secondary school heads have suddenly discovered the wisdom of treating their primary colleagues as valued colleagues rather than as poor relations. Both primary and secondary school heads may increasingly find that they have to persuade parents not only about the academic qualities of their schools but also about the quality of care and guidance they provide.

Second, and following from this, the motivation for the steady stream of legislation since 1980 has not been confined to concern over educational standards. Concern about the social function of schooling has also been a motivating factor ever since the Black Papers of the 1970s attributed allegedly declining standards to the subversive activities of militantly left-wing teachers (e.g. Cox and Boyson, 1977). A succession of papers from the DES, reflecting the government's views, and from HMI have considered what form of personal and social education schools should provide. We shall see later that their views do not always coincide. What is not in dispute, though, is that by the late 1980s personal and social education was attracting more political and professional attention than for many years previously. In the next chapter we consider some of the implications.

Questions and exercises

1. Think of pupils you have taught and/or observed in the last six months and list those whose motivation may be affected by an unhelpfully low opinion of themselves and of their abilities. Now state what you consider to be the most likely reason for each pupil's low self-esteem. Be as specific as you can. 'Backward in all subjects', for example, is not in itself a cause of low self-esteem. On the other hand, continually being compared by a parent, or teacher, with brighter children might be. Role play an interview between the class teacher and parent(s) of one of these children.

Recommended reading

Best, R., Jarvis, C., and Ribbins, P. (Eds.) (1980) *Perspectives on Pastoral Care*. London, Heinemann.

Department of Education and Science (1988) *School Teachers' Pay and Conditions Document, 1988*. London, DES.

Lang, P. (1988) *Thinking about Personal and Social Education in the Primary School*. Oxford, Blackwell.

Maslow, A. H. (1970) *Motivation and Personality*, 2nd edition N.Y., Harper and Row.

Ryder, J., and Campbell, L. (1988) *Balancing Acts in Personal, Social and Health Education*. London, Routledge.

CHAPTER 2

The scope and limits to the teacher's responsibility

Introduction

Any primary or secondary school classroom contains children with a wide range of backgrounds and previous experiences. The children may all belong to the same ethnic group, though this is unlikely in most parts of Britain. They may even all come from the same social class according to the usual criteria of parental occupations, though this is even more improbable. It is virtually certain, though, that they will not all be living with both natural parents. Their families' lifestyles, financial circumstances and religious affiliation will vary, almost certainly widely. The primary school class teacher and the secondary school form tutor will find that parents of some pupils take an active interest in their progress; parents of others regard education firmly as the school's responsibility. Teachers will soon become aware that a minority of pupils live in families which appear to inhibit their personal development and educational progress. They may also find that parents vary in what they expect from the school in terms of behaviour, dress, and personal and social education.

Faced with the diversity and complexity of the pupils' cultural and social backgrounds, it is tempting to take the view: 'We're teachers, our job is to teach, not to worry about their backgrounds'. Unfortunately there are two powerful objections to this. First, it implies an 'hydraulic' model of teaching and learning in which the teachers job is to be present with the jug of knowledge ready to pour into the preferably receptive little pitchers in front of them. Teaching involves an interactive process to which pupils also contribute. A lesson dominated by teacher talk is as dull as a lot of university lectures (without the carrot of a degree after a mere three years' acquiescence). Without some awareness of their pupils' social backgrounds, personality and interests, it becomes very difficult for teachers to motivate pupils to take an active part in their own learning.

Second, teachers have always been concerned with more than the formal curriculum. In the last century Arnold of Rugby School regarded 'character training' and gentlemanly conduct as more important than academic progress. For the first three quarters of this century, the pupils' 'personality development' was often seen as an important pastoral function of schools. In recent years it has become more fashionable to talk of personal and social education.

This chapter examines what is meant by personal and social education. It also considers a slightly different question, namely how far teachers can meaningfully be said to have a responsibility for their pupils' personal and social development. Children's attitudes, behaviour and progress are not only influenced by the curriculum and the way teachers present it. There are many other influences, both at school and at home. One group of influences is contained in the 'hidden curriculum'. We consider briefly the evidence that this has a substantial influence on all aspects of pupils' development at school. The chapter discusses what is meant by the hidden curriculum, and how it can exert a positive or harmful influence. It also considers how teachers' own biases, conscious or otherwise, may affect their behaviour towards children and what they expect from them.

Finally, we look at the extent of a teacher's responsibility for pupils with special social needs, for example pupils who may be subject to neglect or other forms of abuse within their families. We argue that teachers have a responsibility to be observant, and to create a climate in which pupils feel able to approach them with personal problems. They also have to know about, and to notify appropriate agencies outside the school, but this is not the end of their responsibility to the child.

Personal and social education

The concept of PSE

How we define personal and social education depends on what we see as its aims, and this is fraught with controversy. The government appears to see the function of personal and social education as preparing young people to take their place as responsible citizens and employees (e.g. DES, 1985a). This does not always rest comfortably with that of creating questioning, critical, autonomous young people who think and act for themselves, willing 'to resist exploitation, to innovate and to be vigilant in the defence of liberty', as was recognised in a joint DES/HMI document in 1977. Since then differences between the government's perceptions of personal and social education as reflected in DES publications and those of its professional advisers, HMI, have become more marked. There is little doubt that HMI's views reflect the conventional wisdom of professional educators much more closely than do those of the government.

It is worth noting that the concept of personal and social education is politically and morally neutral. It was considered at least as important in Hitler's Germany as in any late 20th Century Western democracy. The point is simply that while different people may agree on the importance of personal and social education, they may have entirely different things in mind, depending on their political, moral and religious values. My aim here and in chapters 3–4 is to demonstrate the importance of adopting a clear position on what personal and social education entails, not to defend any particular position.

In chapter 1, I defined personal and social education as all the learning experiences which give pupils a developing sense of their own abilities and of their rights and responsibilities as contributing members of the school and of the wider communities in which they live. By a 'developing' sense of their own abilities and of their rights and responsibilities we imply simply that pupils' concepts of themselves and of their position in the family, school and society develop with age. How the concept of self develops is the school's responsibility as well as the parents' though tension is likely when parents have differing views on the school's role. Many of the learning experiences which affect pupils' personal and social development are incidental, arising from the school's hidden curriculum. There is nevertheless a strong argument that personal and social education has important curriculum implications which require as careful planning as any other curriculum area. We return to this in chapters 3 and 4. At this stage we need to look at issues which arise from our definition of personal and social education, and at some of the problems resulting from it.

Whose rights and responsibilities?

Logically, we cannot talk about children developing a sense of their rights and responsibilities as contributing members of the school without also considering our own rights and responsibilities as teachers. Asking what children, or their parents, should feel entitled to expect from the school is perhaps one of the most effective ways of setting ourselves high professional standards. There is very little here that we can take for granted. Parents will normally expect that their children should at least recognise their school's head-teacher. Yet in one comprehensive first year pupils were in no doubt about the identity of the begowned figure known to staff as the head teacher who descended to the lower school site once a week to take assembly. He was, they affirmed, the local vicar! More seriously, parents are entitled to expect that their child will be known reasonably well by at least one teacher, and have ready access to this teacher. Yet the organisation of some comprehensive schools makes this virtually impossible.

If we consider seemingly straightforward expectations such as: 'children shouldn't be made to feel inferior by criticism', or 'children should feel that they learn from their mistakes' we can find ourselves in even deeper water. Overwhelmingly, the evidence suggests that a substantial minority of children suffer from increasingly low self-esteem as they progress through the school system. Providing critical feedback which pupils interpret as a way of helping them to master the task in hand, rather than as a negative comment about themselves, is perhaps one of the most challenging tasks for a teacher.

Values and beliefs

Whenever we state what standards we expect from pupils, for example, in dress or behaviour, we are influenced by our own values and beliefs. The problem here is that each teacher's own beliefs and values will certainly differ from those of many pupils and their parents.

Two examples of beliefs are: 'There is but one God, Allah', and 'Jesus is Lord'. Two examples of values are: 'We should respect the religious beliefs of others', and 'we should not make fun of people because they are disabled'. Differences in religious and political belief may be associated with differences in values. Most Quakers, for example, would argue that war is never morally justified. This is a value judgement, derived from their belief that the biblical injunction to turn the other cheek proscribes violence in any circumstances. Other Christian groups do not share this belief, and consequently adopt different values.

In spite of the inter-relationship between values and beliefs, it remains true that no community can flourish without broad agreement on values. Lack of such agreement leads inevitably to anarchy. At school level, the teachers' values are reflected in the behaviour they expect from their pupils, and, more subtly, in what pupils expect from each other and from teachers.

Any school or youth organisation requires a generally agreed, though not immutable, set of values in order to maintain a climate of stability in which learning is possible. It also requires some concept of its own inter-relationship with wider groups. The values which the head and staff seek to promote throughout a school cannot be totally idiosyncratic. If they are rejected, or just not understood, by a majority of parents, no policy on personal and social education is likely to be effective. Another influence, which is still of some importance is that of the LEA. Just as the teachers' values are reflected in the written and unwritten policies of the school, so the collective values of the Education Committee may also be formalised into a set of more or less well defined policies which attempt to influence the values adopted and promoted by teachers.

Notable examples in recent years are anti-racism and anti-sexism policies. Some LEAs have requested each school to produce its own policy to combat racism and sexism. It is important to note that the assumed need for a formal policy to combat these problems implies that the teachers' existing value-systems may tolerate, or even foster, behaviour which discriminates against pupils or fellow staff members on the basis of race or sex. We return to this question shortly. The success of an anti-racist or anti-sexist policy at LEA level in overcoming racist or sexist practices in schools remain a matter for research. What is not in doubt is that what pupils learn in school about personal relationships, with each other and with adults, will be influenced by their perception of their teachers' values. The clarity with which these are formulated and expressed will be reflected in the school's climate and hidden curriculum.

The most far-reaching attempt to influence the values which schools seek to develop has not, however, come from LEAs but from central government in the form of the 1988 Education Act. The introduction of a national curriculum places an explicit value on an organised, and centrally determined body of knowledge, while national testing seeks to develop a competitive ethos within and between schools. The increase in parents' freedom to select their children's school, their greater representation on governing bodies and the local financial management of schools may all be seen as an attempt to increase a sense of parental and community responsibility for what happens in schools.

The hidden curriculum

Concept and definition

The hidden curriculum can be defined as the network of relation-ships in a school, between teachers, between pupils and between teachers and pupils which determine what teachers and pupils expect of themselves and of each other. Both pupils' and teachers' expectations are influenced by the structure of the society in which they live. Authors with a Marxist orientation tend to regard the social and economic division in society as having an overwhelming influence on the hidden curriculum, against which individual teachers are powerless (e.g. Bowles and Gintis, 1976). This deterministic view underestimates the ability both of teachers and of pupils to take independent action in protection of their interests. Nevertheless, it is difficult to under-estimate the importance of the hidden curriculum. It includes all incidental learning and reflects the social and emotional climate of the school. It has been seen as one of the most powerful means by which society defines the value attached to different kinds and levels of achievement, and thereby controls and shapes the behaviour of its future citizens. Until twenty years ago, for example, the classics enjoyed a uniquely high status throughout the secondary school system. Today, their place has been taken by the sciences and new technological subjects. Some subjects are consistently accorded low status by universities and future employers. It is still true, for example, that a pupil wishing to read English at most universities would be better advised to take additional 'A' levels in French and Maths than in Home Economics and Art.

This raises an important question: how much influence can a school's teachers exert over the hidden curriculum? If, as some sociologists seem to argue, the hidden curriculum is the inexorable result of wider pressures in society, then all that teachers can do is bow to the inevitable. Such fatalism is not, however, justified. Certainly, the status which society accords to different subjects will influence examination choice in secondary schools. It will also, more subtly, influence the primary school curriculum. The demands of parents that their children acquire sound literacy and numeracy skills at an early stage can be a powerful influence on teachers who value artistic and creative skills more highly. Similarly, few secondary school governors or heads, are likely to take as much pride in Mr Jones' achievement in teaching three pupils with special needs to read as in Mr Smith's in helping three high-flying sixth formers to win places to read Maths at Oxbridge. Nevertheless the relationships developed within a school are not a simple reflection of those in society. Children's behaviour varies from school to school, and within each school from class to class. The individual teacher has an enormous influence on the social and emotional tone of his or her class. The fact that we talk of the 'hidden' curriculum does not mean that its effects cannot be observed, nor that it is unalterable. In other words, teachers have as much responsibility for the hidden curriculum in their classrooms as for the official curriculum.

The hidden curriculum is too often portrayed as a negative influence, invoked to explain disaffection from school, disruption in the classroom and the development of deviant anti-authority sub-cultures amongst low ability fourth and fifth formers in secondary schools. Yet disruption is by no means a universal problem in primary school classrooms, nor is disaffection inevitable in secondary schools. There is strong evidence that the climate of the school and the effectiveness of the individual teacher have much greater influence on the pupils' relationships, behaviour and general expectations than their social or family backgrounds. In an interesting article Roberts (1979) argues that the hidden curriculum in an infants' school can be a powerfully beneficial influence. She describes how one class teacher acted to prevent a child from being regarded as a problem by the rest of the class, and how other teachers encouraged co-operative work, appreciation of the effort made by a child with particular difficulties, and tolerance of an obese boy. The same principles apply in secondary schools. In some schools bullying is a perennial problem; in others it is a rare event. One head teacher argued against setting up a special group for disruptive pupils on the grounds that this would strengthen their deviant identity. Instead he insisted that all pupils would be taught in ordinary classes, where the pro-social peer group was the most powerful argument against disruptive behaviour.

Prejudice and discrimination

Many of the messages conveyed through the hidden curriculum are unconscious. I know a junior school in which all pupils play soft ball in the summer term. The boys play on the playing field with a solid ball, and the girls on the playground with a soft ball. There is no conscious desire amongst teachers to discriminate against girls. Similarly, very few teachers consciously discriminate against Afro-Caribbean pupils. Yet the evidence from a major research study shows clear evidence of ability banding based on pupils' perceived behaviour rather than their attainments (Eggleston *et al*, 1985).

A commitment to pupil welfare requires understanding of our own biases, and an attempt to understand those of others, though not necessarily to agree with them. Recognising prejudice and avoiding discrimination requires us to look at our own practices from another person's viewpoint. Some teachers continue to adopt a 'low-key' response to racial remarks, preferring not to condemn them forcefully as offensive on the grounds that to do so would give them undue prominence. From a black pupil's perspective, and probably from that of white pupils too, however, this low-key response may be seen as condoning remarks that are deeply offensive.

Prejudice is not confined to racism and sexism. It can be seen in almost all aspects of life, whenever people of different ages, cultures and social classes live and work together. This section identifies five areas of prejudice that frequently affect teachers in their relationships with pupils and with each other.

Sexism

Sexism may be defined here as any practice which discriminates against an individual on the basis of his or her gender. There is an enormous literature on the subject, with ample evidence that both primary and secondary schools encourage stereotyped sex roles on numerous occasions throughout the day (e.g. Marland, 1983; Sutherland, 1981). To take two seemingly innocuous examples, it is virtually universal for boys and girls to hand their coats separately, and for school registers to list girls after boys. In assembly, from the age of five onwards, it remains frequent practice to seat boys and girls separately; being made to sit with the girls, or vice versa, is often used as an effective sanction against talkative pupils. In the classroom, there is evidence that boys attract a disproportionate amount of the teacher's time (French and French, 1984). Indeed, if girls receive their 'fair' share of attention, boys protest forcefully that 'you only ever ask the girls'! The reason probably lies in the fact that boys are more frequently disruptive (e.g. Rutter *et al*, 1979) and hence that they are seen as posing more of a threat to classroom stability and order. Nevertheless, there is an obvious danger that by reinforcing stereotypical male traits, teachers may also be reinforcing a climate in which girls are assumed to be relatively passive.

There are two possible consequences. First, when a girl does behave atypically, for example by refusing to work and preventing other pupils from working, she may be seen as a 'psychological' problem requiring 'treatment' whereas a boy behaving in a similar way may be seen as a 'straightforward' disciplinary problem. The disturbing implication here is that the girl's behaviour is beyond her control, and hence not the teacher's responsibility, whereas the reverse applies to the boy (Dweck, *et al*, 1978).

The second possible consequence also has potentially long-term effects. If girls are seen, consciously or otherwise, as relatively passive compared with boys, and if they attract less of a teacher's attention, this may affect their choice of subjects for public examinations. It may also affect the status accorded to the subjects they choose. It is known that Physics, Chemistry and to a lesser extent Maths are taken disproportionately by boys, whereas languages, English and to a lesser extent, Biology tend to attract girls.

In some schools some subjects are informally identified as 'boys subjects' and others as 'girls subjects'. In theory they are open to all, but the informal messages are quite clear. In this connection one of the central tasks for a secondary school's pastoral work with third year pupils is to ensure that they make informed choices of subjects to study for public examinations. More specifically, are all girls aware of the employment doors that are closing when they opt out of science and technical subjects?

Racism

This refers to any practices or behaviour which distinguish between people on the basis of race. It is illegal in Britain to discriminate against someone on this basis, as on the basis of sex. Nevertheless, there is a wide gap between formal discrimination and a host of practices which can profoundly affect the educational welfare of pupils from minority ethnic groups.

We have already referred to the evidence that Afro-Caribbean pupils are placed in low ability bands on account of teachers' assessments of their behaviour, although in theory selection is based solely on ability. Earlier, Stone (1981) had reported the indignation of many people in the Afro-Caribbean Community that schools tended to identify their children as being particularly good at sport or music. They wanted their children to obtain formal qualifications, and saw the teachers' emphasis on their achievements in the school brass band or sports teams as a diversion from this first priority. The obvious danger is that such extra-curricular subjects may fill the same function as 'girls subjects' – a relatively low status activity compared with the 'important' academic subjects, but a convenient way of giving these pupils a sense of achievement, and thus socialising them into accepting their lot.

The way in which people of minority ethnic groups are portrayed in school reading and text books has attracted a good deal of attention recently. Mercifully few schools now contain copies of Little Black Sambo. Nevertheless, some of the most widely used reading schemes in infants schools still appear to be based on the assumption that all families in Britain are white and middle class. Others, such as the original Pirates schemes only portray black people as the 'baddies'. The situation is, however, changing as publishers respond to pressure to reflect the multicultural nature of modern Britain in their new publications and in re-issues of old ones.

This leads us to important questions about the nature of a multicultural society and about the relationship between a multicultural approach and an anti-racist one. It is sometimes argued that a multi-cultural curriculum is needed only in schools with a multi-ethnic intake. This argument is, at best, highly contentious. The reason is that *all* children, irrespective of where they live, should develop an understanding of the multi-cultural nature of their country, and a respect for the beliefs and traditions of people from cultures other than their own. This, of course, is an example of a value judgement. The idea that teaching, or writing, can ever be value-free simply does not stand close inspection.

If we accept that a multi-cultural curriculum extends beyond teaching awareness of other cultures to include respect for them, we can see why an anti-racist policy becomes a logical necessity. The point is that logically we cannot teach respect for other cultures without identifying and striving to eliminate examples of prejudice and discrimination in our own. In practice this means that we have to start with recognition of our own previously unconscious or taken-for-granted assumptions. If we do not recognise our own biases, we can hardly expect to tackle those of our pupils.

Classism

Probably the strongest and most deeply felt argument against the eleven plus was the disproportionately low number of children from working-class backgrounds who gained grammar school places. Today, parental occupation, the basis of social class divisions, remains a powerful predictor of future educational success. Put simply, middle-class children are far more likely to gain sufficient public examination passes at sixteen, to progress to more advanced study or to enter higher-status jobs in the labour market. The introduction of comprehensive secondary education has not changed this situation. Indeed, some critics would claim that many comprehensives reproduce the old grammar-secondary modern divisions in the way they group pupils by ability (e.g. Reynolds *et al*, 1987).

The question we need to consider here is whether teachers, from the nursery school onward, are unwitting instruments in widening social class divisions. 'Classism', then, refers to any occasions in which a teacher's judgement of a child's behaviour or performance is influenced by the child's social class. This can happen in many ways. Teaching is a middle-class profession and schools, more or less consciously, encourage or require middle-class modes of speech, behaviour and dress. The days have gone when children were taught to chant: ·

God bless the squire and his relations
And help to keep us in our social stations.

Yet primary teachers and their pupils continue to sing, with exuberance, a verse from the hymn All Things Bright and Beautiful:

The rich man in his castle,
The poor man at his gate,
God made them, high or lowly,
And ordered their estate.

Few teachers can say with a clear conscience that they feel no more surprise or concern about the below average reading ability of the son of two doctors than about the similar ability of the son of a council workman and an office cleaner. The tendency to under-estimate the ability of working-class children is widespread at all levels, including nursery schools (Tizard and Hughes, 1984). So, incidentally, is the tendency to expect less co-operation from their parents than they are willing and able to give.

Ageism

This refers to the view that people of a very different age to oneself are hopelessly stuffy and out of date (if older) or full of woolly 'modern' ideas (if younger). It is surprisingly prevalent in schools, seen in the attitude of older teachers to their younger colleagues and, sometimes, to the pupil's parents, and in the attitude of younger teachers to their older colleagues. For the student and newly qualified teacher much depends on estab-lishing good working relationships with the head and senior staff. There is some evidence that this may be more difficult, on both sides, when the age gap is large (e.g. Galloway *et al*, 1985).

There is a parallel here between pupils' use of the school, and the teacher's use of colleagues' experience. A pastoral issue which has received inadequate attention both in primary and in secondary schools is how to help pupils make the best possible use of the school in general and of their teachers in particular. Indeed, using the teacher's time and skills effectively could be considered one of the basic skills which pupils need to learn. We only have to consider elementary skills such as asking for help, learning from mistakes and making use of opportunities outside the classroom to realise that many pupils, especially those with special educational needs, consistently seem unable to use the school effectively.

In exactly the same way, some newly-qualified teachers experi-ence great difficulty in making effective use of the knowledge, experience and skills of their more senior colleagues. We return to the question of work with colleagues in chapter 9. At this stage we need only note: (a) that relationships with senior colleagues are a frequent source of concern to beginning teachers; (b) that the responsibility for relationship problems virtually never rests solely with one party; (c) for this reason, there is a great deal that teachers themselves can do to get a more positive and helpful reaction from colleagues.

Parentism

I am indebted for this term to a London head-teacher (Marland, 1985). It refers to the belief that parents are almost always in the wrong, and should never be permitted to play more than a minimal and token part in their children's education. This would be denied flatly by virtually all head-teachers, yet the practice in some schools suggests otherwise.

Many, though by no means all, infants' schools welcome parents of new entrants into the classroom to help their children settle. Some, but certainly not a majority, welcome subsequent offers from parents to help in the classroom. Junior schools which welcome such help are considerably rarer, though many seek help with outings, and secondary schools virtually non-existent. In Britain, unlike in other EEC countries, parents are asked to take their child's education 'on trust'. The nearest they can get to finding out what actually happens in the classroom is to attend open evenings, to listen to what their children tell them, and to request a special interview after school hours. 'Parents as partners' is a piece of educational rhetoric which is reflected in the practice of no more than a tiny handful of schools. A good test for seeing whether parents are really regarded as partners is to ask whether they would be welcome in the staff-room in the break or lunch hour.

The benefits of involving parents actively in their children's learning at school are well documented. Asking parents to listen to their children reading, for example, has been shown to be more effective than provision of extra teaching from a specialist reading teacher (e.g. Tizard *et al*, 1984). Yet no more than a small minority of schools make an attempt to involve all their pupils' parents in a regular and consistent way. We look in chapter 7 at ways of working effectively with parents. At this stage we need only note: (a) that partnership with parents is more often a matter of rhetoric than of reality; (b) that the reasons for this are deeply embedded in the culture of the teaching profession; (c) that the consequent division between learning that takes place in the home and learning that takes place at school is a major obstacle to effective teaching.

Conclusion: where does responsibility stop?

We have argued so far:
(i) that teachers have a responsibility for their pupils' personal and social education;
(ii) that in consequence, quite apart from any implications for the official curriculum, the class teacher's responsibility includes a commitment to the social climate or hidden curriculum of the class;
(iii) that within each of us there are areas of prejudice and discrimination – the more charitable word is 'biases' – which affect our attitude and our behaviour to pupils and to colleagues;
(iv) hence, that effective teaching requires a high level of self-knowledge from the teacher.

Recognising one's own strengths and limitations is crucial if we are to make an informed decision on when to seek assistance from one of the education or social work support services. The teacher's task is not to replace social workers or educational psychologists, but rather to advise when a member of these services might be able to help a child or parent. Personal contact is invaluable here.

Within the classroom the teacher's task is to create a climate which facilitates effective communication and provides opportunities for it to occur. This has implications for the sort of relationship teachers establish with pupils individually and as groups. Does the relationship help children to seek support from a trusted teacher, or does it encourage them to bear their fear or anxiety in lonely isolation? Facilitating effective communication, though, does not depend only, even mainly, on relationships with pupils as individuals. It also depends on the teacher's interaction with the class as a whole. This takes us to the curriculum.

Questions and exercises

1. Read the prospectus for your school. What values does the school claim to develop? How are these reflected in the way you organise your own classroom?
2. Consider the following three anecdotes:
   (a) At Jimmy's primary school all third and fourth year children play soft-ball in the Summer term. The boys play in the playing field with a solid ball. The girls play in the school playground with a tennis ball.
   (b) In the secondary school all children are supposed to wear uniform, one aspect of which is black leather shoes. When John needs a new pair, his mother says she has noticed children wearing trainers to school, and asks why he won't wear his trainers. 'Oh', says John 'only "B" band kids wear trainers to School'. His observation is, on the whole, accurate.
   (c) An eleven-year-old is loudly rebuked for talking in assembly, and sent from the hall to wait outside the head's office. Immediately before this incident the teacher taking assembly had been delivering a homily about the importance of being nice to one another.
   In each of these incidents, what messages are transmitted through the school's hidden curriculum?
3. Think of incidents you have encountered in your own experience as a pupil or a teacher. Again, what 'lessons' were 'taught' through the hidden curriculum in each of these incidents? How might the teacher have handled the situation differently?
4. This chapter identified five areas of possible prejudice and

discrimination. The first three are well known. The last two have attracted less attention but may be just as pervasive. All of them may affect your effectiveness as a teacher. Taking each of the five areas in turn, think of examples, in the behaviour of colleagues *and* of yourself from your last teaching practice or your last term teaching. How has your own experience as a pupil and in your family influenced your current attitudes?

Recommended reading

Banton, M. (1988) *Racial Consciousness*. London, Longman.

Bowles, S. and Gintis, H. (1976) *Schooling in Capitalist America*. London, Routledge and Kegan Paul.

Department of Education and Science (1985) *Better Schools*. London, HMSO.

Marland, M. (1983) *Sex Differentiation and Schooling*. London, Heinemann.

Stone, M. C. (1981) *The Education of the Black Child in Britain*. London, Fontana.

Tizard, B. and Hughes, M. (1984) *Young Children Learning*. London, Fontana.

CHAPTER 3

A curriculum for PSE: aims and issues

Introduction

Chapter 2 introduced the concept of the hidden curriculum and its effect on pupils' personal and social development. This chapter will explore the relationship between the 'official' curriculum, the hidden curriculum and classroom teaching processes, and will discuss the somewhat nebulous notion of school ethos in relation to its effect on pupils' personal and social development. We shall argue that a commitment to pupils' welfare in general, and in particular to their personal and social development, have curriculum implications, and identify some of the issues on which all schools, whether they acknowledge the fact or not, have an influence.

Influences on the curriculum

The content of the official, or stated curriculum contains messages which are transmitted through the hidden curriculum. This is seen most obviously in the status attached to different subjects. Parents may be disappointed if their children show little ability in creative arts but they will be seriously worried if progress in Maths and English is demonstrably unsatisfactory. Science and Maths may have replaced Latin and Greek as the most prestigious subjects on the curriculum, but the relative importance attached to Home Economics and Art remains low in most schools. This differential status is further emphasised in the importance attached in the national curriculum to science and technical subjects. This bias is even more pronounced in the government's initiatives for the 14–19 age group. In considering the effect on pupils' personal and social development, it is interesting that subjects carrying high status such as Maths, Physics, Chemistry and technological subjects consistently attract more boys than girls in the 6th form and in GCSE courses. The reverse is true of subjects such as modern languages, Home Economics, and to a lesser extent English and Music. The hidden curriculum message here is that gender equates with status (e.g. Manthorpe, 1982; Whyte *et al*, 1985).

A more obvious influence on the hidden curriculum in schools lies in the organisation of the education system itself. The existence of the private sector draws explicit attention to the power of money to buy what parents see as educational privilege. For parents and for children, it is a short and very easy step from believing that the education at the local primary or comprehensive is unsatisfactory to concluding that the children at these schools are less desirable as friends. The introduction of city technical colleges and grant maintained schools may produce the same divisiveness with the state system as already exists between state and independent schools. In theory city technical colleges will admit pupils from the full ability range, and grant maintained schools will not initially be able to change their present character. In practice the power of head-teachers and governors over admissions may well ensure that children will be turned away when they, or their parents, are deemed to be backward, inarticulate, unco-operative, or to have special needs which might threaten the stability and standards of the school. In fairness, this at present appears less probable in grant maintained schools than in city technical colleges. The lessons transmitted through the hidden curriculum will be damaging for the personal and social development of comprehensive school pupils *and* of their more privileged peers who gain places in the more generously resourced city technical colleges or in grant maintained schools.

The School's Influence

Individual schools are constrained by the national curriculum, though in practice this is by no means the straight jacket which it is sometimes alleged to be. It would be naive, though, to pretend that the pupils' background and their parents' expectations will have no effect on how the national curriculum is taught. Moreover, divisions within society and within the education system also exert an influence on the hidden curriculum, and hence on what pupils learn about themselves, each other and society during their school careers. It would be easy to conclude that teachers have little influence over their pupils' personal and social development. They are stuck with a national curriculum, imposed by a government in which no cabinet minister sends his or her child to a state school. Even in grant maintained schools, they have limited influence over admission of pupils, and none at all over the organisation of the education system nor over divisions within society. This pessimism is not justified. Research on school and teacher effectiveness has not looked specifically at the effects of schools as institutions or teachers as individuals on pupils' personal and social development. It has, however, produced indirect evidence suggesting that the effects are considerable.

The most well known British study of school effectiveness is that of Rutter *et al* (1979). The authors followed the progress of pupils through twelve Inner London comprehensive schools. They made allowances for differences between schools in the pupils' educational attainment on entry and in social class, as measured by parental occupation. After taking these into account they found important differences between the schools in the pupils' attendance, in the proportion of pupils known to the police for delinquent activities, in their examination results and in their behaviour within the school. The school's influence was strongest, though, on the pupils' behaviour within the school. A similar result was found in a study of junior schools in Inner London. Mortimore *et al* (1988), and Galloway et al (1989) have reviewed and have reported further evidence that the school's influence on its pupils' behaviour is as great, and probably greater, than the influence of catchment area factors.

By comparison, the school's influence on its pupils' personality development has received less attention. However, Dyer's (1968) reanalysis of a major American study (Coleman *et al* (1966) suggested that schools varied in their pupils' sense of control over their own lives and the ILEA study claimed that junior schools exerted a substantial effect on their pupils' self concepts. In addition, Rutter *et al* (1979) reported that the more successful schools made greater efforts to involve pupils in decisions affecting them. There was a strong tendency both in this study and in Mortimore's junior school study for teachers in the more successful schools to maintain control through reliance on praise for achievement rather than on rebukes and sanctions.

Further research has shown that the differences between teachers in their effects on pupils' progress are greater than the differences between schools. Bennett (1976), for example, compared teachers who were using mainly formal methods, teachers who were using informal methods and a 'mixed' group. He found that different teaching styles had less effect on pupils' progress than individual teachers, irrespective of style.

Similarly Newbold (1977) concluded that whether teaching groups were ability-based or mixed ability mattered less than the role of the individual teacher. Observation in both primary and secondary schools also confirms that pupils' behaviour varies very widely from class to class. Some teachers have serious discipline problems and pupil motivation appears low. Others succeed in creating a pleasant and business-like atmosphere in which almost all pupils take a pride in their work. Clearly, differences between classes of similar ability *within* a school cannot sensibly be attributed to catchment area or family factors.

It is one thing to claim that schools and teachers have a major effect on their pupils' behaviour, but quite another to argue that they have a similar effect on their personal and social development. Part of the difficulty lies in the fact that although everyone agrees that schools should have a responsibility for pupils' welfare in general, and for their personal and social development in particular, there is no consensus on the definition of these terms, let alone on how they can be measured. However, the picture that emerges from a review of research on school effectiveness is that some schools, and some teachers in all schools, succeed in creating a climate in which disruptive behaviour is infrequent, pupils feel actively involved in the social and educational life of the school and teachers expect, and receive, high standards of work and behaviour. However we decide to conceptualise personal and social development, it would be odd to deny that these factors are relevant. The question, then, is how some schools generate in pupils a feeling that their achievements and opinions are valued while others are conspicuously less successful.

It is clear that the hidden curriculum provides important learning experience which cannot be irrelevant to personal and social development. However, the hidden and the official curricula interact with and influence each other. Hence, we also need to consider whether a commitment to personal and social education has implications for the content and/or teaching of the official curriculum.

Can there be a curriculum for personal and social education?

The inevitability of personal and social development

When talking about personal and social education we normally imply that the outcome will be beneficial both for the individual and for the society in which he lives and works. Unfortunately education does not always have 'positive' outcomes. Children are not born with a sense of failure and personal inadequacy, but these can be acquired as a result of their learning experiences at home and at school. The concept of development implies that changes occur as a result of maturation and of experience. It does not imply that the change is in the direction predicted or desired by teachers, parents, the LEA or the government. In chapter 2 we defined personal and social education as learning experiences 'which give pupils a developing sense of their own abilities and of their rights and responsibilities as contributing members of the school . . .'. This refers to *all* learning experiences which affect pupils' ideas about their own abilities and about their rights and responsibilities. It implies nothing about *how* their learning experiences will affect them.

This point becomes clearer from consideration of David Hargreaves' (1982) penetrating attack on much contemporary schooling. He claims that the secondary school system, mainly through the hidden curriculum, exerts on many pupils: 'a destruction of their dignity which is so massive and pervasive that few subsequently recover from it' (p.17). The principal victims, according to Hargreaves, are working-class children. Yet the picture he paints is not altogether bleak. He identifies ways in which pupils succeed in preserving their self-respect. These include formation of anti-authority sub-cultures in which respect is earned by opposition to the school's rules and values, and by an explicit assertion of their own values in such matters as dress, music and leisure activities. There can be no doubt, if Hargreaves is correct, that these pupils' personal and social development was heavily influenced by their experiences at school. The fact that they were not influenced in ways that their teachers intended, nor of which society would have approved, is irrelevant to the argument that they *were* influenced.

It is not only teachers who can avoid seeing the potentially negative effects of personal and social education through the hidden curriculum. Until quite recently all forms of sex education in primary schools in New Zealand were illegal, and the Minister of Education rejected the recommendation of a government committee (N.Z. Department of Education 1977) that it should be introduced into the curriculum. The law was carried to ridiculous lengths. When a teacher caught boys giggling over a pornographic magazine he removed the magazine and discussed with the class the negative way in which it portrayed women. A parent complained and he was dismissed. What no-one involved in this charade, least of all the Minister, seemed to recognise was that sex education has always taken place in primary schools, in New Zealand and everywhere else. It can be made illegal within classrooms, but this merely ensures that it continues to take place furtively, with no guidance from teachers, in the playground, the toilets and the bicycle sheds. Moreover, the pupils' recognition that no aspect of human sexuality may be discussed in the classroom is itself a powerful, if negative, piece of education about sex.

Pupils' personal and social development, then, is influenced not only by the ethos of the school as a social community but also by their teachers as individuals. Indeed, schools cannot operate without providing personal and social education, simply because they are social communities. The question is how it occurs, and with what result.

Another curriculum subject?

Recent years have seen a proliferation of materials for personal and social education programmes. An obvious stimulus for them has been the rapid development of pastoral care networks in secondary schools, and recognition of the form tutors' need for a programme of activities if pupils are to be known and valued as individuals in large comprehensive schools. Probably the most widely known schemes are Button's (1981) *Group Tutoring for the Form Teacher*, and Baldwin and Wells' (1979) *Active Tutorial Work*. Baldwin and Wells were greatly influenced by Button's work, and the two schemes have a number of common features. The most important of these are their provision of a programme of activities for each year group aiming to promote personal growth. The activities are seen as a way of offering pupils:

. . . opportunities for vital experiences with other people, through the membership of supportive groups who are learning to help one another in personal ways.

(Button, 1981, Book 1, p.2)

Most secondary schools in England and Wales have purchased copies either of Button's books or of Baldwin and Wells'. Both urge that their programme should be seen as a coherent whole, and prefer teachers to use the full range of activities for their pupils' age-group. Yet although most secondary teachers with pastoral care responsibilities know of these schemes, my experience on numerous INSET courses in pastoral care and tutorial work suggests that they are very seldom used in the way the authors intended. There seem to be three inter-related reasons.

1. The relationship between the tutorial programme and all the other activities of the school and with the rest of the curriculum is not always clear; consequently, many teachers see it as an additional chore that is, at best, peripheral to their main responsibilities.
2. The authors, particularly Button, seem to assume a distinction between group work in tutorial groups and 'ordinary' subject teaching. Certainly, teachers often feel that they are being expected to acquire a new and different set of skills rather than build on their existing skills. This is in fact probably a false assumption. Primary teaching requires many of the group-work skills demanded in these programes. In addition, the GCSE curricula for many subjects also require similar skills in group work and in active learning techniques to tutorial activities. Nevertheless, it is clear that both the tone of the books and the nature of some activities alarm many teachers.

3. Perhaps as a result of the first two points, the activities are often seen as having low status. It is still unusual for a school to specify in the further particulars for an advertised post that the successful candidate will be required to take a form tutor group in addition to subject teaching responsibilities. All too easily, tutorial work, and implicitly a commitment to personal and social education, is seen as a peripheral chore. When this happens, it does not just mean that no personal and social education programme is provided. It means that pupils receive a clear message about their form tutor's priorities, and hence about the value they should attach to different aspects of their experience at school.

Any published programme for personal and social education runs the risk of being regarded as a 'bolt-on' attachment with no implications for the rest of the curriculum. In fairness, both Button and Baldwin and Wells recognised this possibility. Yet providing a time-tabled programme of activities reinforces, almost inevitably, precisely this limited concept of personal and social development. Change, as they would probably be the first to admit, is usually resisted unless it develops from a perceived need from within. Both in secondary and in primary schools, the core activities lie, and have always lain, in what is now the national curriculum. Hence, this also provides the core experiences for personal and social education. Nevertheless, as we explain in the next chapter, there will still be a need for additional programmes in secondary schools and for planned activities which may not readily be seen as part of the national curriculum in primaries.

This statement has two implications. First, much of what is taught as part of personal and social education should explicitly be integrated into appropriate areas in the national curriculum. Second, and more difficult, the social climate in classrooms throughout the school must be one which facilitates the school's overall aims with respect to pupils' personal and social development. This requires a separate discussion.

A permeation model?

Theoretically, the idea that everything that happens in school, both in the official curriculum and in the hidden curriculum, contributes beneficially to pupils' personal and social development is an attractive one. The question is simply how we reach this happy state of affairs. Primary teachers sometimes express pained surprise at the suggestion that the personal and social education they provide should even be a matter for discussion: 'But you don't seem to understand; everything we do is concerned with this. You can't talk about it in isolation; it's part of the whole classroom experience.'

This is fine in theory. Too often, though, the practice reveals personal and social education that is indeed all-pervading, but in precisely the negative and destructive way that has so frequently been documented in secondary schools (e.g. Hargreaves, 1982, p.17). Sex stereotyping, for example, may recur on numerous occasions throughout the day (Whyte, 1983). Children may be grouped around tables according to ability, and rapidly develop ideas about their respective status. Even the often quoted claim that they work in co-operative groups is highly questionable. They may sit in groups but research shows that in most class-rooms, children spend most of their time working individually (Bennett *et al*, 1984).

The assumption that this whole area is unproblematic prevents a clear analysis of ways in which schools affect their pupils' personal and social development. These include the development of gender and ethnic identity, feelings of selfworth and attitudes towards competition and/or co-operation with others. In secondary schools there is the additional problem that if personal and social education is considered to be everyone's responsibility it can all too easily become no-one's. In other words, if no-one has responsibility for providing an overall sense of direction on the grounds that everyone is 'doing' PSE, an overall sense of direction is likely to be lacking.

Personal and social education across the curriculum?

A starting point for understanding personal and social education is to examine how, and in what ways, different curriculum areas contribute to it. There is a parallel here with language. The Bullock Report (DES, 1976) popularised the concept of language across the curriculum. The old cliché that all teachers in English are teachers of English is none the less true for being a cliché. Yet the fact that all teachers have a responsibility for language development, in all areas of the curriculum, makes careful thought and planning more necessary, not less. Further, the fact that everyone is involved merely underlines the need for a teacher with specific expertise in the area to provide a school policy, and regular in-service work-shops on implementing this policy.

The same argument applies with respect to personal and social education. It is precisely because all teachers have responsibility in this area that schools need a clearly defined policy and a senior member of staff to take responsibility for implementing it. In primary schools this may be the head or deputy. In secondary schools a deputy head usually co-ordinates the pastoral team of heads of year or house. Almost all teachers in secondary schools have explicit responsibilities as form tutors, so each head of year will be responsible for co-ordinating the work of a team of tutors. We consider in more detail how the teams may function most effectively in the next chapter.

Towards a consensus on issues covered in PSE

Problems in defining aims

Personal and social education is provided through the official and hidden curricula in schools. Logically, then, it is impossible to talk of aims for personal and social education without reference to the varied influences on these curricula. Influence can be exerted at several levels. The government is now taking an extremely active and prescriptive interest in the curriculum, and within government imposed constraints, LEAs are developing their own curriculum policies. The school's governors, and in a less co-ordinated way its pupils' parents, may also exert an influence both on the content of the curriculum and on teaching methods. Within a secondary school individual departments usually have a degree of autonomy, for example on matters such as ability grouping. Finally, but by no means least, the individual teacher is, and should be, able to interpret the school's and department's policy in a flexible way.

The problem is that the individuals or groups who influence the curriculum conceptualise the aims of personal and social education in different ways. A DES/HMI (1980) report, for example, talks about pupils forming 'an acceptable set of personal values' (p. 2). They do not, because they could not, define what personal values are 'acceptable'. The reason is that acceptability is determined by the prevailing beliefs, and the values associated with beliefs, within particular communities.

Ideas about right and wrong do not exist in a vacuum. In western countries, for example, the belief that bigamy is wrong is endorsed by the law. In other countries bigamy is permitted not only by the law but by religious belief. Even if we think of apparently uncontroversial value-statements we quickly run into trouble. Where, for example, does respect for the views and values of others stop? Would the government, or even school governors, have been happy about schools teaching respect for the Argentine position during the 1982 conflict? More recently the government's move to make it an offence for schools to teach positive images of homosexual behaviour illustrates how 'respect for others' can be a politically and morally contentious matter (Local Government Act, 1988).

It follows that any set of general aims for personal and social education will reflect the values and moral priorities of the people who hold them. Since so many diverse individuals and groups have legitimate, but conflicting interests in the school curriculum it would be tempting to conclude that no agreement is possible. Yet that would be a recipe for inertia, which everyone would agree is not desirable. Moreover it ignores the point, argued earlier, that *all* pupils' experiences at school will have an effect on their personal and social development. This, however, suggests a way out of the dilemma.

PSE as an intrinsic aspect af all education.

We have already argued that schools cannot function without reference to moral values. At the most superficial level these are reflected in the school's rules of pupil behaviour. Only a bit less obviously, they are reflected in the climate teachers try to create in their day-to-day responses to events in and out of the classroom. Children learn what their teachers regard as socially acceptable or unacceptable behaviour. As important, they also learn what other pupils consider acceptable or otherwise.

A related issue is that teaching is impossible without recognition of individual differences. These include not only differences in ability and educational attainments but also in family income, social class, gender and ethnicity. Thus, if a school has rules about uniform it will have to decide what to do about pupils who turn up not wearing it. The rules may be intended to disguise social class differences, but if, as is not infrequently the case, the pupils who arrive 'improperly' dressed come disproportionately from disadvantaged homes, the school's response cannot avoid teaching all pupils something about divisions within society. Exactly *what* is learnt will depend on the responses, but that something will be learned is indisputable.

Indirectly, pupils will also learn something both about the role of the school in its local community and about the value which teachers place on their parents' part in the process of education. In a minority of schools parents are seen, and see themselves, as equal partners with teachers. This implies that teachers learn from the parents' knowledge of their children and provide opportunities for active involvement in the life and work of the school. A more frequent pattern is to preserve the curriculum as the 'secret garden' which parents may not enter, though the 1980 and 1986 Education Acts and the 1988 Education Reform Act are changing this picture.

So far, we have been talking about learning that takes place through the hidden curriculum. The official curriculum, too, will necessarily have an impact on pupils' personal and social development. Thus, in providing guidance for option choices for a GCSE course teachers will inevitably convey something about the status attached to different careers. This can have far-reaching implications, not least in view of the evidence about gender disparity (Kelly *et al*, 1984, Whyte *et al*, 1985). Whether this occurs in spite of guidance offered by teachers or because of it, is not for the moment the point. Further, careers education does not start in the third year of secondary schools. In infant and junior schools children start to learn about the world of work, both from their teacher's approach to her work and from her attitude towards other occupations which crop up during day-to-day classroom activities.

Another obvious curriculum area with implications for personal and social development is health education. It is not possible to teach Home Economics or PE without reference to hygiene. Nor, in spite of the practice in some Roman Catholic schools of teachers cutting offending pages from text books, is it possible to teach biology with no reference to reproduction. Pupils may not be *taught* anything more about health education in the curriculum than that it involves care of the body. If so, they will neverthelss *learn* that certain issues are taboo and cannot or must not be discussed, at least in school. With the growing threat of AIDS, this attitude is changing, but what is taught, and how, remain subjects of intense controversy.

Finally, even if the school has no course in civics or citizenship as such, pupils will learn something through the curriculum about the organisation of society in a democracy. This may well occur in discussion about general elections and local by-elections. It can also arise spontaneously in primary school projects and in secondary curriculum areas such as History or environmental studies. Education about politics is a contentious area, though. Feeling with some justification that they are on dangerous ground, many teachers confine themselves to basic facts about elections. This is a pity. McGurk (1987) found that fascist parties such as the National Front were exerting an influence on growing numbers of 16–18-year-olds. Indeed, the only party political policy which some were able to identify was the enforced expulsion of non-whites. All too easily, children can be fed the bland diet satirised by Tom Paxton in the 1960s in his song, 'What did you learn in school today?':

I learned that policemen are my friends,
I learned that justice never ends,
I learned that murderers die for their crimes,
Even if we make a mistake sometimes.

Parliament has not yet decided to risk repeating this particular mistake. Yet in spite of the evidence on the extensive use of 'stop and search' powers by the police, and on the resentment engendered particularly amongst young black teenagers, few schools risk incurring the wrath of politicians and other local worthies by discussing with pupils the scope of police responsibilities and powers, let alone of their own rights when stopped. Pupils are more likely to learn that topics such as this which concern them directly, on which they have strong feelings and about which they are often ill-informed, are simply not considered relevant in the school curriculum.

Developing a policy

Both the formal and the hidden curriculum, then, provide experiences of immediate relevance to children's personal and social education. They will learn both from what they *are* taught and from what they are *not*. The process of schooling, like experience in the family and experience in other settings, will influence pupils' feelings about themselves, each other, the world of work and the environment in which they live. It will help to shape their concepts of right and wrong. It will extend or restrict their ideas about their rights and responsibilities and about the contributions which they can or should make to the life and work of the school.

Since we know that children will learn *something* in these areas, it seems logical to develop a policy which will influence *what* they learn. Establishing a policy on personal and social education will have implications for the content of the official curriculum. It will also have implications for the social climate which teachers wish to encourage in their school, and hence for the hidden curriculum. This will not ensure that children learn what we intend them to learn, but it will provide a clear set of values to follow in formulating objectives.

An obvious objection to this argument could be the impossibility of formulating universal aims for personal and social education. The fact that individuals and groups differ in their values yet have legitimate, but conflicting, views about the school's role in personal and social education does not mean that the school can avoid having a policy. Indeed the health of a school depends on adopting and maintaining a clear set of values. Developing a policy for personal and social education requires a school to formulate aims which are generally acceptable to the staff. This has two consequences. First, the general aims must be translated into specific questions: what do we want children to learn, and which teaching methods are most appropriate? Asking these questions implies the need for a critical review of each curriculum subject's contribution to personal and social development. Second, a school policy demonstrates the teacher's sense of professional accountability to the managers or governors, and through them to their pupils' parents.

Conclusions

We have argued in this chapter that any general set of aims for personal and social education can be attacked, since aims are derived from beliefs and values, about which disagreement is both extensive and legitimate. Teaching is not and cannot be value-free, since pupils are affected both by what teachers do and by what they avoid doing. Children are not born with a ready-made personal identity. It develops in a social context, and after the family, the school probably provides the most influential social experience for children and adolescents. Since personal and social education occurs in school, it is a matter on which teachers cannot avoid having a policy. The next chapter discusses models for planning and implementation.

Questions and exercises

1. How do the values transmitted to less able pupils through the hidden curriculum differ from those transmitted to academically able pupils? How much can the school do about this?
2. In what ways does the curriculum experience of boys and girls differ in your school?
3. List all the occasions in which boys and girls are required to do things separately in a typical school day. How much of this differentiation is necessary?

Recommended reading

Hargreaves, D. H. (1982) *The Challenge for the Comprehensive School, Culture, Curriculum and Community*. London, Routledge and Kegan Paul.

Hulmes, E. (1988) *Education and Cultural Diversity*. London, Longman.

McPhail, P., Ungoed-Thomas, J. R. and Chapman, H. (1972) *Moral Education in the Secondary School*. London, Longman.

Mortimore, P., Sammons, P., Stoll, L., Lewis, D. and Ecob, R. (1988) *School Matters: The Junior Years*. Wells, Open Books.

Rutter, M., Maughan, B., Mortimore, P. and Ouston, J. (1979) *Fifteen Thousand Hours. Secondary Schools and their Effects on Pupils*. London, Open Books.

CHAPTER 4

A curriculum for PSE: planning and teaching

Introduction

The last chapter identified issues which, for better or worse, will affect pupils' personal and social development at school. Any experience of living and working with other people will have an effect on a person's personal and social development, whether adult or child. Hence, this is an area in which teachers will have an influence and on which schools need to develop a clear policy with aims and objectives agreed by the staff and by the governors. No policy is likely to be effective unless class teachers in primary schools and subject teachers in secondary feel that they have been actively involved in producing it. Nor will it be effective without broad agreement on the classroom teaching processes which will help to meet the policy's aims and objectives.

This chapter considers the problem of deciding what learning experiences relevant to personal and social development should be provided in each curriculum area. We then consider a model for planning the personal and social education curriculum in primary and in secondary schools. Finally we discuss aspects of classroom teaching which seem particularly relevant to personal and social education.

Curriculum content

Identifying issues of particular concern in personal and social development does not tell us what to teach. A conventional but still useful way to start thinking about this is to ask what facts we think pupils need to know, what attitudes we want them to develop, what skills we want them to learn and what concepts or understanding we want them to acquire. We will also need to consider what experiences we want to provide for pupils in helping them to acquire the facts, attitudes, skills and concepts that are identified in each area.

These divisions are, of course, arbitrary and overlapping. It is impossible to develop any understanding about something without knowing any facts about it. Acquiring a skill also requires knowledge of factual information, even when referring to skills in inter-personal relationships. Some pupils antagonise teachers by not using appropriate social skills. For example, failure to make eye contact can lead to the pupil being perceived as devious, even though in some cultures it is considered rude for a child to make eye contact with an adult, especially in disciplinary situations. Children can be taught this skill, but it clearly contains a factual element.

On the other hand, knowledge of facts does not necessarily imply the skills to make effective use of them, nor does it necessarily imply anything about the attitudes a person will hold. Indeed, attitudes are notoriously independent both of factual knowledge and of behaviour. Someone may behave in a highly prejudiced manner towards people of minority ethnic groups, yet hold tolerant, 'liberal' attitudes. The converse is also true, and can be seen in racist attitudes held by children who nevertheless willingly work and play with members of a different ethnic group.

It cannot be too strongly emphasised that the facts, skills, attitudes and concepts that teachers wish to encourage will vary from school to school. This is evident from consideration of health education, a curriculum topic which does not form part of the national curriculum, but for which the government considers schools to have some responsibility and which has obvious implications for the present discussion. In infant schools there may not, at first sight, be too much controversy. Teachers wish to teach children the importance of bodily hygiene and the reason for it. Some children will need to be taught basic skills such as washing their hands and brushing their teeth, (although many schools would not regard the latter as their responsibility). Yet even here there can be controversy. The attitudes that teachers think children should acquire towards their bodies are an important aspect of health education but are strongly influenced by religious belief. The attitudes that are regarded as important in a Roman Catholic infants' school may not be the same as those held in the state-maintained school a hundred yards down the road.

If we consider topics that may be introduced in the later primary school years disagreement becomes more obvious. Sex education is often seen as an aspect of health education, though it can also form part of other curriculum areas. The 1986 Education Act imposed on governors the duty to decide whether sex education should be provided, and if so in what form. Thus, decisions on whether children should be taught about human reproduction and if so, at what stage and with what audio visual resources (e.g. the BBC schools television programmes) will depend on the nature of the school, governors' perceptions of the local community and, not least, teachers' own feelings of competence. By the secondary school years, disagreement has potentially reached the stage of intense controversy. Decisions have to be made on whether to teach about contraception, and what, if anything, to teach about AIDS and other sexually transmitted diseases. We say 'if anything' because in spite of the proliferation of materials for use in schools and the government's expressed view that pupils should be given information about AIDS (DES, 1987a, b), there is no consensus within the profession as to whether or how this should in fact take place. To take a specific example, teachers in some schools may feel: (a) that no teaching about AIDS is possible without explicit reference to high-risk practices and high-risk groups, such as anal intercourse between homosexuals; (b) that pupils should be shown with a model the correct use of condoms. In other schools reference to any birth control technique would be considered totally inappropriate, as would any reference to anal intercourse. There will be similar lack of agreement on the attitudes which schools seek to develop. Some seek to encourage tolerance of and respect for differences in sexual orientation. Others regard all forms of sexual activity outside marriage as morally wrong and see it as their duty to make this view clear to pupils.

The principal problem in published sex and health education programmes is the difficulty they face in catering for the legitimate differences in opinion as to what should be included. In referring to 'legitimate' differences, we are, of course, making a value judgement. For some religious groups it is a cardinal principle that their views represent God's, and that any deviation from this must be sinful. This intolerance is matched by some secular groups who wish similarly to impose their view that any behaviour between consenting adults is socially and morally acceptable.

Clearly, all of this requires a statement of the position adopted in each school and broad agreement on the facts, skills, attitudes and concepts which teachers think children should acquire. Without this broad agreement the next stage is difficult if not impossible. This involves planning an outline health education curriculum for each year group. These outlines can then be put together in the form of a 'map' showing the development of health education throughout the school's age range – infant, junior or secondary. This ensures both that the curriculum for each year group is age-appropriate and also that there is a logical development from year to year. It enables teachers to see how their work with a group of children fits into a wider programme. It also enables teachers to inform governors and parents about this aspect of the curriculum, to seek their reactions and ultimately to enlist their support.

Health education is only one aspect of the curriculum for

personal and social education. Other areas covered through the official curriculum are potentially as controversial. Thus, developing an age-appropriate understanding of the world of work sounds fine until we consider the logical problem that seeking work implies the possibility of unemployment and the practical problem that occupational choice in the area may be severely restricted. At an only slightly more complex level, it raises questions about differences in wages, salaries and status between occupations. From here it is only a short step to considering the morality of employment policies, and of both management and trade union practices. We could take things one stage further still. All teachers would agree that theft is wrong. But does this extend to 'theft' of an employee's time and skills by paying a wage below the recognised poverty line or in working conditions that infringe the various employment acts? Through the Council for Accreditation of Teacher Education, the Secretary of State for Education and Science requires all initial teacher training courses to equip students to teach an understanding of the world of work. One wonders whether this was what he had in mind.

Nor are we on much safer and less controversial ground in other areas of obvious relevance to personal and social education. Teaching children an awareness of and respect for the neighbourhood of the school, and the leisure activities provided in it sounds uncontroversial and commendable. If the locality has demonstrably been damaged, for example by destruction of hedgerows, pollution from a factory, or unimaginative housing developments with inadequate services it is no longer uncontroversial. If the managing director of the factory responsible for the pollution is the chairman of the Education Committee and a local MP, or if the farmers who pulled up the hedgerows are parents of children in the school, or if two of the councillors responsible for the housing development are governors of the school it becomes explosively controversial.

Any attempt at education about political processes is fraught with similar dangers. Teachers will almost certainly agree that it is none of their business to impose their own political beliefs on pupils. Yet an attempt to explore ways a citizen may legitimately influence political decisions in a democracy can lead straight into controversy: What forms of protest are acceptable? What rights do pupils have to make their voices heard? If they disagree with a decision of the local council – the teachers' employers – what can they do? Which pressure groups have been successful in the past, and what methods did they use? Does violence ever succeed as a form of political protest? If so, is it ever justified? If not, how many of Britain's former colonies would have achieved independence? There are no right or wrong answers, but any attempt to teach pupils about politics may run into deep water if questions of this sort have not been carefully considered.

So far we have been discussing ways in which aspects of the official curriculum may contribute to pupils' personal and social development. Equal attention is needed to learning that occurs through the hidden curriculum. Crucially, this includes relationships – between pupils, between teachers and between teachers and pupils. Again, bland statements about mutual respect sound fine until we look at them a little more closely. Relationships between pupils and teachers cannot be seen in isolation from the concepts of authority and of power. Because they are in a position of authority, teachers have power. It does not follow that they should or will behave in an authoritarian way, but it does mean that children will learn something from their teachers about power relationships. These are expressed in their most negative form in Raymond Garlick's disturbing poem, Thug:

School began it
There he felt
The tongue's salt lash
raising its welt

On a child's heart.
Ten years ruled
by violence left him
thoroughly schooled,

nor did he fail
to understand
the blow from the
headmaster's hand.

That hand his hand
round the cosh curled,
what rules the classroom
rocks the world.

Even if we comfort ourselves by dismissing the pessimism in this poem as atypical – and most educational psychologists could think of young people whose delinquent career started in the way suggested in this poem – it remains true that the child's concept of authority is strongly influenced, for better or worse, by contact with teachers. It also remains true that teachers disagree, sometimes radically, on what constitute 'appropriate' relationships between them and their pupils. To take two extremes, some believe that in matters of morality, behaviour, dress, and school rules they should neither expect nor countenance discussion. Within the Christian church different groups interpret the Bible in their own way, and some at least demand unquestioning obedience to their beliefs. The same applies within Islam to interpretations of the Koran. These absolutist beliefs are reflected in the view of some schools, and of some teachers in many schools, about relationships between teachers, people in authority, and pupils, over whom they have authority. At the other extreme, A. S. Neill (1937) ran his school Summerhill on the principle that children could question anything, and would be jointly involved with teachers both in formulating the rules and in responding to transgressions.

Complete agreement between teachers in a school on the relationship between themselves and their pupils is neither realistic or desirable. It is not realistic because teachers are no more uniform in their beliefs and values than any other group of people. It is not desirable because children need to learn to recognise and cope with diversity. A school in which all staff behaved with the absolute consistency advocated, apparently, by some behaviourists would provide poor preparation for future life. It would also be suffocating. There is nevertheless a need for broad agreement within a school on the sort of relationships teachers wish to develop with their pupils.

We have argued that the process of formulating the school's concept of personal and social education has implications for the official curriculum and for the social and emotional climate of the school. This may require clarification of the school's values and some difficult decisions on what should be taught in order to support these values. We must now consider how this might be achieved.

Planning the PSE curriculum: primary

Individual or joint responsibility?

A planned programme for personal and social education is particularly necessary in primary schools for two reasons. The first is the traditional autonomy of the primary class teacher. The second is the prominent place in the primary curriculum of project and topic work. A programme for each year group is needed; (a) to avoid omitting issues which teachers and governors consider important; (b) to avoid duplication; some issues will be repeated in consecutive years, but not at the same level; (c) to ensure a broad consensus on what the school is trying to achieve with respect to personal and social education. This implies the need for a school programme on personal and social education, just as for Maths, English, Science and other subjects in the national curriculum. The question is who should be responsible for planning this.

Three principles appear important. First, to ensure coherence

and development across the age-range, the head or an experienced nominee will need to convene a small group of teachers
to produce the outline programme referred to earlier. This will
identify issues which should be covered in the course of the year.
Second, the class teacher will retain responsibility for deciding
how they should be covered, and at what stage in the year. In
other words the personal and social education programme will
provide clear guidelines on what should be covered, but will not
override the class teacher's autonomy by undermining the flexibility which characterises good primary teaching, allowing the
teacher to incorporate a wide range of curriculum experiences
into work on a project or on a particular theme. Third, the fact
that class teachers retain this autonomy implies the need for guidance and support from an experienced colleague. Under the
teachers' new conditions of service (DES, 1988a), all teachers may
be expected to develop an area of specific expertise. Given its
complexity, it seems logical that one teacher should be given
responsibility for developing expertise in personal and social
education. A major purpose in requiring all teachers to develop
an area of specific expertise is, of course, to facilitate and extend
school based INSET. This does not mean that the main task of
the teacher involved in personal and social education will be to
provide sessions for the whole staff on INSET days, though this
may be desirable from time to time. It does mean that he or
she will be available on a day-to-day basis for discussion with
colleagues on ways to incorporate aspects of the year's personal
and social education programme into the projects or themes on
which children are currently working.

Planning the PSE curriculum: secondary

Some background considerations

Two aspects of secondary education present particular difficulty
in planning a programme for personal and social education. The
first is the subject-based nature of secondary education. The
second is the development of pastoral care networks in which the
heads of year or house enjoy similar status to heads of subject
departments. The subject divisions are self-evident. As we
argued earlier, all teaching has implications for pupils' personal
and social development, but in some subjects they are more
immediate than in others. It is difficult, for example, to imagine
teaching English Literature without explicit discussion of
relationships between people, nor to imagine PE teaching
without reference to health education and to pupils' awareness
of individual differences in physical co-ordination.

Planning a curriculum which, by definition, crosses subject boundaries, presents the obvious problems that teachers will vary widely both in their understanding of personal and social education and in the importance they attach to it. Some heads of department encourage their colleagues to teach in a way that encourages social awareness. Others consider themselves bound by the letter of the curriculum and see no need to step outside it. To take one example, the concepts of science and of computer technology are morally neutral. Science can be used for the benefit or the destruction of humankind. Computers can be used to guide missiles in the final world war or to provide a more fulfilling life for disabled people. An imaginative teacher can introduce science or technology in a way that extends children's understanding of its practical application and potential benefits. Given the popularity of 'space invaders' and similar computer war games which implicitly equate the use of computers with aggression, this appears particularly desirable.

Problems arising from variation between teachers in their understanding of personal and social education can be compounded by the way a school organises its pastoral care network. This is by no means inevitable. We do, however, need to recognise some of the practical and theoretical problems in pastoral care.

Pastoral care or social control?

In the selective system of education, heads and deputy heads of grammar and secondary modern schools undertook responsibility for pupils' welfare. As long as schools remained small this was perhaps manageable, but with the introduction of much larger comprehensive schools it was no longer credible. It became apparent that a formal structure was needed to cater for pupil welfare. Pastoral care may not have been invented by comprehensive schools, but they were certainly responsible for placing it on an institutional footing. Head teachers and governors started to appoint heads of year or house, and a career ladder was created in parallel to the ladder leading to headship of a subject department.

Why and how this happened is a matter for debate. The conventional wisdom of pastoral care holds that its origins reflect the influence of the public school system with its emphasis on character training (e.g. Best *et al*, 1980). This may be an over-simplification. It is cynical but not unrealistic to point out that posts of responsibility for pastoral care provided 'consolation prizes' for heads of department in former secondary modern schools when their former grammar school equivalent was appointed head of department in the new comprehensive. Today, pastoral care continues to provide an alternative career ladder for teachers who are unable, or do not wish, to obtain promotion as head of a subject department.

Yet this was probably not the main factor in the growth of pastoral care networks. Comprehensive schools, by definition, required teachers to cater for a much wider ability range than the previous selective system. Teaching, in other words, was becoming more difficult, and teachers felt that behaviour problems were increasing. It is doubtful whether this was in fact the case since the evidence from the 1920s and 1930s suggests that behaviour problems then were at least as prevalent and as severe as they are now (Galloway *et al*, 1982). On the other hand, parents were probably expecting more from the education system by the 1970s and teachers were certainly more aware of the needs of their less able and less co-operative pupils. The 1969 Children's and Young Persons Act was creating, or perhaps reflecting, a climate which regarded problem behaviour as a symptom of personal or family disadvantage. At the same time professional and public opinion was becoming increasingly critical of sanctions such as corporal punishment which had seldom previously been questioned. Pastoral care networks, then, could easily be seen as a response to the new comprehensive school's need for control in the increasingly liberal climate of the 1960s and 1970s.

However, this analysis presents both theoretical and practical problems. The theory, or perhaps simply the rhetoric, of pastoral care emphasised its function in the school as a caring community. The reality, as Best *et al* (1983) demonstrate in their detailed study of pastoral care in one school, was concerned with matters of organisation such as lunch-time passes, supervision of bus queues, and behaviour. In many schools, pastoral care came to be equated with penal care, since heads of year were routinely responsible for investigating and dealing with cases of disruptive behaviour. Experience on INSET courses for pastoral heads shows that this is a continuing pattern.

It does, however, raise two problems. First, the belief that disruptive behaviour can be 'cured' by counselling from a head of year, or from anyone else, is naive and unsupported by evidence. Indeed the evidence from studies of the effectiveness of counselling and psychotherapy suggests that disruptive pupils are much less likely than most other pupils with problems to benefit from this form of intervention (e.g. Levitt, 1963; Robins, 1972; Mitchell and Rosa, 1981). The second problem is more pragmatic. Giving heads of year responsibility for investigating and dealing with problem behaviour surrounded the role of other teachers in ambiguity. Subject teachers were nominally responsible for discipline in their classrooms, yet a colleague at 'middle management' level also had responsibility. Teachers who might have hesitated to refer a problem, such as chewing gum in class, to the head teacher for fear of appearing ridiculous had much less compunction in passing it over to a less senior colleague who might lack the confidence or the status to tell them to sort it out themselves.

The role of the form tutor was surrounded in even greater ambiguity. One function of the pastoral network was to ensure that every pupil had a point of contact with at least one teacher. It was unrealistic to expect a head of year to know all pupils in the year group well; there might be as many as 300 in a large school. Consequently, the form tutor would be the basic unit of pastoral care. Because pupils might be taught by as many as ten teachers in the course of a week, and because each subject teacher might see as many as 500 pupils during the week, the form tutor was the only practical person to whom responsibility for getting to know a small group of pupils well could be delegated. Unfortunately, while this was recognised in theory its practical implications were not.

In discussing research projects in fourteen secondary schools in Sheffield, UK, and in New Zealand, Galloway (1983) noted that all head teachers acknowledged form tutors as providing the basis for pastoral care; yet the organisation of pastoral care in many of these schools made their role virtually impossible. This could happen: (a) because they changed tutor groups each year, thus making continuity of care difficult; (b) they only saw their tutor groups for ten minutes each day and consequently felt that their main responsibility as form tutors was the low grade clerical chore of completing the register; (c) they did not teach their subject specialism to pupils in their tutor group, and therefore lacked the opportunity this might have given to get to know the pupils in a different context; (d) the year tutor's job was defined in terms of investigating and dealing with problems, with the result that form tutors felt that pastoral care was their responsibility, and the form tutor's role was to refer problems to them.

This rather depressing scenario was not evident in all schools. Indeed, it was at least in part as a result of growing recognition of problems in the concept and practice of pastoral care that academics and practitioners started to develop tutorial activities which might give the form tutor a more constructive role within the pastoral care network (e.g. Button, 1982; Baldwin and Wells, 1979). We have already argued that these programmes, while perhaps useful and important in themselves, are limited by their focus on the work of form tutors. Personal and social education has much wider implications for the curriculum and for the social climate of the school. Although this was never the authors' intention, a programme of activities for form tutors could all too easily equate personal and social education with tutorial activities, thus reducing it to the level of a marginal activity and confirming a spurious distinction between the academic curriculum and pastoral activities.

There is something more than faintly futile about a form tutor's use of activities designed to develop trusting relationships (for example a blindfolded pupil being guided round the room by another pupil) in a school in which trusting relationships are conspicuously lacking. The futility lies not in the activity itself, but in the naive view that an activity which is inconsistent with everything else that is happening in a school can compensate for its shortcomings. One does not have to be an experimental psychologist to recognise problems of learning transfer and to know that skills acquired in one context, whether academic or social, are unlikely to generalise to other contexts unless opportunities are provided for practising them.

If this analysis is correct, it follows that tutorial activities should build on and extend the best of the social and educational learning which takes place in the rest of the school. In schools which have developed trusting relationships and in which effort is valued as highly as achievement, many of the more personally challenging activities in tutorial programmes will be both appropriate and useful. This is not however, always the case. The question, then, is how to plan a curriculum for personal and social development which recognises the importance not only of form tutor, but also of the mainstream curriculum.

Two stages in curriculum development

In their study of twelve London comprehensive schools, Rutter *et al* (1979) noted a tendency in the more successful schools for heads of department to involve their colleagues in planning the curriculum. In these schools, teachers did not have complete autonomy over what they taught, since curriculum planning was a joint responsibility. This also has implications for planning the school's programme for personal and social education.

As in primary schools, an outline programme for each year group is needed. The hierarchical structure of secondary schools, together with the way pastoral care is organised, suggests that a deputy head might convene and chair a working group consisting of the five heads of year. The group would have two tasks. First, they would need to focus on the programme's content. This will vary from school to school, but there are core issues which will require attention. These include careers education and pupils' understanding of the world of work, health and sex education, study skills and their ability to make effective use of resources available in the school, awareness of their rights and responsibilities in the local community and in the wider society, relationships within the school and outside it. The programme will need to ensure that the major areas contributing to personal and social education are covered, and that there is an age-appropriate development from year to year. This constitutes the basis for a curriculum for personal and social education.

The next stage is perhaps more difficult and involves translating the curriculum into a programme: who will be responsible in each year group for each area of the curriculum? Clearly, certain subject departments are likely to make a major contribution, for example biology, home economics and PE in health education. Planning is needed, though, to ensure that the school's system does not restrict access to parts of the curriculum to a minority of pupils. Planning is also needed to avoid duplication, for example, pupils being shown the same sex education film twice in one week, (a complaint a pupil once made when I asked him why teachers were complaining about his behaviour). The extent to which each subject department contributes to the personal and social education programme will depend on its strengths and limitations. It will also depend on its priorities. Thus, the Geography curriculum is likely at some stage to include study of aspects of the local community. How far this can extend to analysis of social issues will vary from department to department, depending both on the teachers' skills in discussing potentially contentious issues with children and on the way they view their subject.

As well as identifying areas of the programme which would best be covered in subject departments, the planning team will need to consider how to make best use of specific expertise within the school. It seems wasteful, for example, for a careers specialist to spend a lot of time with each third year class providing basic information about the option system that could perfectly well have been provided by form tutors.

A further point is that some areas within a PSE programme may be thought to require specialised teaching. The planning team may recognise that the expertise of particular teachers would best be used in addressing issues with which many other teachers would feel uncomfortable. Matters of personal and sexual morality are an obvious example. Hence, there may be a case for a PSE course which would be seen as forming part of an overall programme.

The tutorial programme will now consist of those aspects of the personal and social education programme which are not to be covered in subject departments nor in a PSE course. This does not imply negative criteria for identifying issues for the tutorial programme. In considering aspects which can be covered by subject departments the planning team will need to balance the time available for tutorial work against an assessment as to whether a particular tutorial team, for example first year form tutors could handle a topic more or less effectively than a particular subject department, e.g. Geography or Home Economics.

Thus, the planning team provides an outline programme for each year group. The tutors in each year group form the tutorial team, co-ordinated by the head of year. Their task is to translate the tutorial programme into a syllabus, specifying in greater detail the topics which will be tackled at different stages throughout the year.

One way to tackle this is to divide the year's programme into a number of themes, and allocate each theme a proportion of the total number of tutorial periods. This will vary from school to school, but most schools time-table between one and three form tutor periods a week. The next step is to plan the content for sessions within each theme. Activities from published tutorial programmes may be useful. Schools Television produces a wide range of programmes that can be invaluable in tutorial work. They include *Tutorial Topics, Scene*, and series on anti-racism, study skills, careers guidance and health education. For some themes visiting speakers may be appropriate.

Dividing the year's programme into themes and deciding how many sessions to allocate to each theme is an activity for the whole tutorial team, though not necessarily a lengthy one. Planning sessions within a theme need involve no more than one or two tutors, with back-up support from the head of year. Thus, if two tutors undertake to plan four sessions for a theme on use of leisure, they will produce an outline for each session, with suggested activities. These will then be duplicated for use by the other form tutors. Few subject teachers will want, or be able, to plan all tutorial sessions themselves. They should, however, be able to produce plans for two or three a term. Circulating these for use by colleagues develops a sense of accountability within the team, since no-one will want a reputation for producing inadequate or boring material. If every member of the tutorial team accepts responsibility for producing plans for two or three sessions a term, excessive demands are made on no-one, but everyone makes a significant contribution to the programme.

Clearly, this model calls for a high level of co-ordinating ability from the head of year. It also requires the head of year to be well informed about resources on which individual or pairs of tutors may draw when planning their sessions. It does not, however, require the heads of year to do all the work themselves. Indeed, if the tutorial team is to function effectively it is essential that every member should not only contribute to the programme, but be seen to be contributing. In other words, the head of year's task is to create an ethos in the tutorial team in which teachers regard tutorial activities as an important part of their work.

Conclusions

We have argued in the last two chapters that PSE has implications both for the curriculum and for the school's social climate. The hidden curriculum affects pupils' personal and social
development, but it is a fallacy to believe that teachers have no
influence over it. PSE demands a clear articulation of the school's
values, since without planning, no PSE programme is possible.
Planning the programme should not be inordinately time-
consuming and brings coherence to a collection of activities such
as health education and careers education which take place in
some form in all schools. In secondary schools tutorial activities
form part of the programme, but no more than part. By influencing the content and process of teaching in the main curriculum
areas, the PSE programme helps to create a positive school ethos
in which high educational expectations do not obscure an underlying atmosphere of trust and respect between teachers and
pupils.

Question and exercises

1. Working with 2 or 3 colleagues, select a curriculum area in
   which you have a particular interest, and review the contribution which it makes to pupils' personal and social
   development.
2. Drawing on your own experience, consider the view that children learn as much from what is *not* taught in health education
   as from what *is* taught.
3. Plan a personal and social education programme for the year
   group you know best. Then compare your programme with a
   colleague's.

Recommended reading

Department of Education and Science (1987) *Sex Education at School*
  (Circular 11/87). London, DES.
Hargreaves, A., Baglin, E., Henderson, P., Leeson, P. and Tossell, T.
  (1988) *Personal and Social Education, Choices and Challenges*.
  Oxford, Blackwell.
Marland, M. (1980) The Pastoral Curriculum. In Best, R., Jarvis, C. and
  Ribbins, R. (Eds.) *Perspectives on Pastoral Care*. London,
  Heinemann.
Neill, A. S. (1937) *That Dreadful School*. London, H. Jenkins.
Ribbins, P. (1985) *Schooling and Welfare*. Lewes, Falmer.

CHAPTER 5

Pupil welfare and classroom teaching

Introduction

It is rightly acknowledged in schools that concern for pupils' overall welfare requires sensitive awareness of personal or family circumstances that may affect a child's motivation or adjustment at school. This is hardly controversial. We argued in the last two chapters that a commitment to personal and social education also has curriculum implications which cannot be satisfied simply by adding a PSE programme to an already over-crowded time-table. A curriculum for personal and social education is an integral aspect of pupil welfare. Clearly, though, the teacher's responsibility for pupil welfare goes further than this. In the course of any lesson children may raise or allude to matters of personal importance ranging from choice of options to acute family problems. This chapter discusses the teacher's responsibilities for creating a climate in which pupils are able to raise sensitive issues, for recognising them when raised, and for responding to them. We are concerned here with classroom teaching. Some children need to be seen individually, either to follow up a matter that first comes to light in the classroom or to talk about something that has occurred outside the classroom. Interviews of this kind are discussed in chapter 6.

Teaching or counselling?

We have already argued that children quickly learn what behaviour is and is not acceptable to different teachers. 'Shadowing' secondary pupils for a day and observing how their behaviour differs as they move from subject to subject, or rather from teacher to teacher, can illustrate this, as can the change in the behaviour of a primary class following a change of teacher. Yet by influencing their motivation and behaviour, class-room climate necessarily also exerts an influence on pupils' moral development. They learn, for example, about the limits to their responsibility to help others. In some formal situations helping others will be regarded as cheating. This is inevitably the case in formal tests which, with the introduction of a national curriculum, seem destined to play an increasingly prominent part in school life from the earliest years.

This will not necessarily preclude development of a co-operative ethos in learning situations. A defender of testing could even argue that it teaches children to discriminate between behaviour which is appropriate in different contexts. They will nevertheless learn something about the values of their teachers and indeed of society. What they learn will depend to some extent on the nature and purpose of testing.

It is still too early to comment on the form this will take. The Task Group on Assessment and Testing (DES, 1988b) believed that the major purpose should be diagnostic and formative. The Prime Minister objected on the grounds that the report placed too much responsibility 'on teachers' judgements and general impressions' (Surkes, 1988). Implicitly, she believed the main purpose of national testing should be normative, to compare children, classes in a year group, schools and LEAs. Designing a test to provide normative data *and* diagnostic information on which to plan future work with a child is a technically difficult exercise. What is not in serious dispute, though, is that the nature and purpose of testing will influence children's development in areas unrelated to the topics of the tests themselves.

Children learn very quickly what behaviour is acceptable and what is expected in terms of co-operative relationships. They also learn about topics which can and cannot be discussed. Some can be discussed openly in the classroom, others furtively in the playground and others kept firmly to oneself. How far children feel able to share their experience in the classroom depends on the teacher and on the 'moral climate' of the classroom. Consider the following poem seen on the wall of an infant school:

We love to squeeze bananas
We love to squeeze ripe plums
And when they're feeling sad
We love to squeeze our mums.

This particular school served an urban catchment area in which most children lived in stable, caring families in which the mutual enjoyment of each other's company implicit in the poem was the norm between parents and children. In Assemblies at this school there was frequent reference to thanking God for the children's families and for the happy times they had with them. Prayers were said for unhappy children, but they always seemed to live either in Ethiopia or in some other part of the country.

For a minority of children at this school, and for a much larger number in other schools, the sunny, idealised picture of family life portrayed in Assembly and in some of the poems on classroom walls bore no relation to their own experience. More important, there seemed to be little or no acknowledgement that the norm did not apply to all children in the school. It might not apply to children in other countries or other schools, yet acknowledging this seemed likely to increase the emotional isolation felt by children whose own experience was different. The emotional isolation could not be articulated, but for these children whole areas of experience could not be expressed in school.

This explains how teachers can sometimes be so woefully ignorant both about their pupils' family circumstances and about their reactions to these. It also explains why teachers and other professionals were for so long apparently unaware of the problem of sexual abuse of children. There is no sound evidence that this problem has increased in prevalence over the last few years, even though more cases are coming to light now than previously. The reason, almost certainly, is that growing awareness of the problem is creating a climate in which it can be talked about, and in which teachers and other professionals are becoming more sensitive than before to indirect cues from children and adolescents that it may be happening. There is an obvious parallel in other areas. How easily, for example, can a child tell a teacher about being locked in his room for hours on end when all the teacher's references to family life in the classroom or in assembly are to happy experiences, and everyone is regularly required to thank God in Assembly for their happy family home.

Teachers' talk, then, reflects their values, which in turn will reflect their own experience and their perception of what are 'suitable' topics for discussion with children. Teachers' talk can encourage children's expression of their personal experiences, or it can have an inhibiting effect. If the children's family backgrounds differ radically from one's own, it may be more comfortable not to know too much about them. Similarly, teachers who have always felt uncomfortable in discussing sexual matters, will feel threatened by references to sexuality from pupils. In each case, the teacher is likely, perhaps without realising it, to create a climate which divorces pupils' experiences in school from their experiences outside.

In one sense this is inevitable. It is not part of a teacher's task to pry into a pupil's private life. Nor is it the teacher's task to induce pupils to share aspects of their private lives which they wish to keep to themselves. On the other hand, enabling pupils to interpret the curriculum in terms of their own experience *is* part of effective teaching. At a very simple level this is seen in primary Maths when children learn the meaning and value of money. At a more complex level, discussion of relationships in a novel or poem can act as a trigger both in primary and secondary schools to extend a pupil's understanding of relationships in his or her own family. Thus, creating a climate in which pupils can articulate their concerns is an important part of the teacher's task.

In discussing the poem printed two pages ago the reaction of one primary teacher was: 'Well what *are* we to do? Just because some children don't come from loving families, we can't base everything we do on them!' In one sense they were undoubtedly right. Schools which have not established a collective set of values and teachers who are uncertain of their own personal values inevitably lack any clear sense of direction. The 'moral' messages they convey to pupils will be arbitrary and conflicting. The fact that many children in a school live in caring, stable and statistically conventional families with mother, father, 1.4 siblings and a cat, provides numerous opportunities for linking their experiences at home and at school, especially in the primary phase. It is clear that to belittle these children's experiences, however indirectly, would be wholly unjustified. It would also be wholly unjustified to belittle the experience of children in less conventional families with a solo parent, or with a parent who is now living with a partner of the same sex. In the same way, while encouraging children to appreciate the warmth and support that most of them receive at home, we should also leave open the possibility that some of them may feel they have little for which to be thankful. Not to do so will belittle these children's experience, and by so doing may create a barrier that prevents them from obtaining from the school the understanding and support that might enable them to cope with the tensions in their families.

Pupils' 'messages'

We must turn now to some of the ways in which children may alert a teacher to personal needs, and consider how the teacher's response may either help a child, or, less happily, create further problems. An example that will be familiar to most teachers is behaviour that might be called 'attention seeking'. This may take the form of 'silly' or provocative remarks, asking frequent questions to which the child already knows the answers, calling out without putting his hand up, getting up and wandering around the classroom and so on.

Not infrequently, the behaviour starts at a time of stress, for example, when the pupil does not understand something, or when concentration and motivation at school are affected by factors outside the school. These could be as minor as a late night, or as major as the parents' marriage breaking up. In most cases a conscious decision by the teacher not to give the behaviour attention, coupled with an equally conscious decision to help the pupil achieve success in the class' regular work, and hence positive attention, is all that is needed. Sometimes, though, the teacher's attention to the problem behaviour, together with the response of other children serves to re-inforce it. This is how many children gradually acquire a role within the class which can interfere both with their own learning and with that of their peers. Two of the most common such roles are the clown of the class and the bully. All too early children can get locked into these roles. Simply trying to ignore the 'clown's' behaviour may then threaten his status within the class, with the possible result that he starts to behave in ways which cannot be ignored. Similarly, a purely punitive response to bullying may reinforce the bully's 'macho' image and thus strengthen the very behaviour it is designed to reduce.

The problem described here is not simply that the teacher's response is ineffective. Worse, the response actually aggravates the problem. The initial response from the teacher gives the pupil a reputation, or role, both in the teacher's eyes and in the eyes of other pupils. The pupil thus acquires an anti-social identity which is maintained both by adult and peer expectation and by the pupil's inability to see how to establish an alternative identity. This process is known to sociologists as secondary deviance, but can equally well be explained in terms of reinforcement principles. Helping the pupil to establish a different role involves the teacher both in finding ways to reduce the anti-social or attention-seeking behaviour and in teaching the pupil alternative, and for the teacher more desirable, ways to obtain attention.

It is important, though, to recognise that children sometimes hide their anxiety about personally sensitive matters behind a façade of flippancy or disinterest. An extreme example of this was provided by a sixteen-year-old boy who appeared quite unnaturally and uncharacteristically cheerful one morning. He laughed, cracked jokes and seemed to have far more energy than usual. At break another boy, obviously worried and puzzled, asked a teacher if he knew Pete's father had died the previous night. Pete's behaviour emphatically did not reflect delight at his father's death, nor even relief, since it had been sudden. Meeting the same teacher again some five years later, Pete told him that his father's death had been the most devastating event of his life.

In a less extreme form similar sorts of reaction are not uncommon in any classroom. They can conceal embarrassment, anxiety or resentment. When reading a story to the class about two children whose father had died, the teacher noted that one usually responsive girl appeared to 'switch off' and had an almost 'frozen' look on her face. In contrast, a boy who usually contributed little appeared uncharacteristically interested. The fathers of both children had died in the previous two years. Another teacher, was surprised by two children's reaction in a lesson on human reproduction. One boy seemed to enjoy shocking everyone with his precocious but not always accurate sexual knowledge. He was the youngest by five years of a large family living in a small tenement flat in which privacy was impossible. A girl in contrast appeared upset but refused to say anything in reply to questions. Six months later her mother told a social worker that she was being sexually abused by her teenage step brother.

In each of these cases the teacher was alert to the child's reaction. The boy whose father had died made no attempt to hide the fact that this was why he enjoyed the book. Knowing that his teacher recognised this provided an important form of support. The girl agreed to a gentle question at the end of a lesson that the book reminded her of her own dad. Asked if she would like to talk to someone about this, she slowly nodded her head. The teacher, quite reasonably, did not feel she had the knowledge or the skill to help this child herself, but was able to arrange to put her and her mother in touch with someone who did have the necessary expertise.

Discussion with the boy living in an overcrowded family showed that he was in fact both puzzled and anxious about the sexual talk he picked up from his older brothers and about the activity he heard and saw. His teacher talked to him later in a down-to-earth, matter-of-fact way about the lesson, to his obvious relief. The girl who had appeared upset in the sex education lesson presented a more difficult problem. The teacher felt that she had insufficient evidence to justify detailed questioning, and thought that this would in any case be unsuccessful. She did, however, mention the incident to the family's social worker who was thus alerted to the possibility of sexual problems in future work with the family.

We must mention one final group of 'indirect' messages which call for particular sensitivity on the teacher's part. These refer to the ways children express their anxieties through the curriculum, for example in their paintings, poems and essays. A ten-year-old drew a picture of a house, divided in the middle by the large figure of a boy. At the time he felt himself, with some justification, to be in the middle of a family dispute in which his parents were arguing not only about his custody but also about which parent should continue to live in the house. A fifteen-year-old girl with a white mother and an Afro-Caribbean father drew a self-portrait of herself looking into a mirror. She painted herself as white, but the mirror image was black, perhaps reflecting her doubts about her own ethnic identity. In an essay a thirteen-year-old boy wrote about a London taxi driver who took the wrong turning on holiday, drove over a cliff and was killed. His father was a taxi driver, and used to punish him severely for the most trivial offences. In another essay an eleven year old girl wrote about a one year old baby being slapped and left in its cot in the back yard because it wouldn't stop crying. She had a baby brother. There was no suggestion of neglect or ill-treatment in the family. The girl was fond of her baby brother – most of the time. Yet there were also times when she resented the noise he made and the amount of her parents' time he took up.

The last example illustrates the danger of reading too much into work that might superficially appear to tell the teacher something about children's family lives or about their private world. It is unusual for an older child *not* to feel strong resentment of a baby brother or sister from time to time. That such resentment is expressed in their writing at school is not surprising, nor even particularly noteworthy. If the teacher already had reasons for concern about the girl, either from her behaviour or from knowledge of previous problems in the family, her essay might legitimately have increased her concern, and might have justified discussing with a more experienced colleague whether or not to contact one of the social work or LEA support services (see Chapter 8).

It is important to be clear about the teacher's responsibility when children's work appears to reflect tensions in their personal lives. There are three crucial points: First, teachers are paid, and expected by pupils, to teach, not to act as psychologists or psychiatrists. Hence their principal responsibility is to react to the quality of the work, as they would react to any other work the child did. Second, both the meaning and importance that the child attaches to the work may be entirely different from the teacher's interpretation. Most teachers have neither the time nor the training to explore with children individually the meaning and importance they attach to something. Trying to do so runs the risk, at best, of confusing the child and at worst of helping children to articulate a problem with which they are then quite unable to cope. The thirteen-year-old who wrote about a London taxi driver's fatal accident always talked with great, perhaps excessive, affection about his father. The fact that he coped with his feelings of anger by appearing to deny them should not obscure the fact that the denial *did* help him to survive in a home which was often acutely stressful.

The third point follows from this. Children's work seldom, if ever tells a teacher, nor a psychologist or psychiatrist, the exact nature of a problem. At best, it may hint at the problem. The teacher's responsibility, then, is to recognise the possibility that children's work may contain hidden 'messages' about matters of personal significance to them. Recognising such messages requires a sensitive awareness of children's personality and relationships in school as well as of their family circumstances. Responding to such messages may require no more than the appreciation normally accorded a piece of conscientious and sensitive work. Sometimes a discussion with a more experienced colleague or with the school's educational psychologist may be useful. Sometimes, too, it may be helpful to provide further opportunities for the child to explore, and hence to clarify, similar themes in the future.

Direct messages

We have been talking so far about indirect messages in which children's work or behaviour in the classroom alerts the teacher to problems either in the curriculum or in a child's personal life. The fact that tensions at home can affect progress or adjustment at school should not obscure the fact that the great majority of classroom behaviour problems arise directly from factors within the classroom. These include the 'testing-out' of any new teacher, not understanding something, feeling that the lesson is dull, perhaps with justification, and so on. Nor should the fact that children's work occasionally draws attention in quite valid ways to matters of great personal sensitivity obscure the point that the great majority of imaginative and creative work is stimulated by experience which is *not* a source of great anxiety or concern. Finally, the fact that children can convey personal information indirectly, should not obscure the fact that any lesson may trigger discussion of events in the pupil's life out of school. Galloway (1976) gives an unusually dramatic example in his case history of Nigel, age 11. The class had just seen a BBC Schools Television sex education film:

After it, Miss Robson asked the class: 'How many of you have baby brothers or sisters?' About six children put their hands up, but not Nigel. 'Nigel has, too, Miss' chimed in Alfred, helpful as ever, especially when there was a chance of stirring things up a bit. Miss Robson asked Peter, a confident self-sufficient boy, how he had felt when his sister was born. 'Fed up!' replied Peter with a cheerful grin, 'She was always yelling, but she's alright now Miss'. Some of the others told the class how they had felt, and then Miss Robson asked Nigel. He shrugged his shoulders non-committally – 'All right' he answered briefly. 'I reckon he was jealous, Miss, because his mum was busy with the baby and hadn't got so much time for him! Hey, What's that for?' Nigel had thrown an exercise book at Alfred's head, and was now standing up, white with anger, more animated than Miss Robson had ever seen him. 'You sod, I wasn't', he shouted (p. 101).

Here, a barbed remark from another child, already noted for his ability to stir things up, touched a raw nerve in Nigel whose mother sometimes kept him at home to look after his baby brother. On one occasion the baby had nearly fallen into the fire when alone in the house with Nigel. The uncharacteristic force of Nigel's reaction alerted his teacher not only to the possibility that the younger brother might be at risk of neglect, but also that Nigel himself had strong, if confused feelings about the situation. This was a time when further discussion on an individual level could have been necessary.

Children's needs

The assumption so far has been that teachers can foster effective communication with pupils on matters of their personal and social welfare. We argued earlier that the mere fact of attending school will affect a pupils' personal and social development, for better or for worse. It follows that one aspect of effective teaching must be concern for pupils' personal and social needs.

The concept of need, however, is far from straightforward. We cannot say we need something without in some sense also wanting it. Even if we say we need an operation but dread having it, we can hardly deny wanting treatment for whatever condition we suffer from. The problem is that children's needs are defined not by children but by adults. In other words, when talking about children's personal and social needs we are talking about what *we* want for them. Inevitably this is heavily influenced by culture and by prevailing ideology on the nature of childhood. Personal and social education is concerned, amongst other things, with the personal attributes which teachers consider desirable. When talking about welfare needs, we are talking, amongst other things, about the experiences from which we think children ought to be protected. This is illustrated by changes in attitude towards corporal punishment. As recently as 10 years ago, many independent schools would have suffered a sudden drop in numbers if they had publicised a policy of never using this sanction. Indeed, parents sent their sons to famous public schools in the knowledge *and expectation* that they would be liable to beatings from senior pupils which, today, the courts would undoubtedly regard as sufficient evidence of child physical abuse to justify removal from home if inflicted by a parent. Similarly, few teachers would claim to wish to develop a spirit of unquestioning obedience to adult authority in their pupils. Yet in some cultures this would rank high amongst the aims of personal and social education.

Our view of children's needs, then, is the product of cultural assumptions held by adults. Teachers do not always share the cultural assumptions of their pupils' parents. Moreover, teachers themselves will often differ in their cultural assumptions, as will parents. To a limited extent, legislation and official guidelines from LEAs and the DES provide a framework for teachers' welfare responsibilities. Yet this framework will be of limited use if teachers lack a coherent set of values on which to base their day-to-day work in the classroom. Some welfare needs, for example signs of physical abuse, may be identified in PE or swimming lessons. Whether the 'abuse' is 'reasonable punishment' is a culturally loaded question, but it will not be the teacher's responsibility to make this decision, since all LEAs have guidelines for reporting all cases of *suspected* non-accidental injury (see Chapter 8).

Welfare needs which occur much more frequently arise from problems such as financial hardship in the home, temporary or prolonged tension between parents, bereavement, and lack of satisfactory alternative care after school hours when both parents are working. The teacher's awareness of these will depend largely on the 'moral climate' which he or she creates in the classroom. It is a central theme of this book that the moral climate of the classroom, and indeed of the school as a whole, cannot be left to chance, but should be articulated and planned. In doing so we have to avoid the trap of relapsing into meaningless platitudes. Perhaps the best example is the often-quoted aim in school prospectuses that all pupils should achieve their 'full potential'. It is unclear whether anyone has ever achieved their full potential, let alone how we could tell whether a child had achieved it. On the other hand conventional staff-room wisdom holds that some children – mainly middle-class – are under excessive pressure from ambitious 'pushy' parents. Presumably these children are being pressurised to achieve more than their full potential. Nevertheless this kind of carping critique should not obscure the importance of attempting to articulate the climate we wish to create. Teachers in one school agreed that they aimed to create a climate in each classroom in which:

(a) all pupils expected, and were expected, to contribute actively to the day's work; one aspect of this was that *all* pupils, irrespective of ability, were expected to produce work of sufficient quality to form part of the displays on the walls and in the corridors;

(b) each pupil's personal experience was regarded as important by the teacher and by other pupils; this implied that:

(c) children gradually developed a more sophisticated awareness of, and respect for, individual differences, one aspect of which was that:

(d) their personal and social development was not restricted by negative labels imposed by peers or by teachers.

This list can, of course, be criticised either because it is incomplete or because the balance is controversial, with its emphasis on personal experience rather than group membership. More-over, regarding personal experience as important and developing a more sophisticated awareness of individual differences are slip-pery concepts. On the other hand, it is possible to observe how far individual pupils are contributing to the work of the class. It is also possible to observe their level of tolerance or intolerance towards individual differences. One measure of this is the preva-lence of derogatory names for less able pupils, for example 'thicko', 'spas', 'divvy'. At least these teachers had agreed criteria for monitoring the social and moral climate in their classes.

The most important point, though, was recognition that this climate should form the background to all the learning that took place in the curriculum. There is little point in talking about how to develop effective communication between children and teacher on personally sensitive issues if we have not established effective communication on more routine matters. From a teacher's point of view, the starting point for their responsibilities concerning their pupils' welfare must lie in their management of the day-to-day business of the classroom. The paradox is that this requires a perceptive understanding of individual pupils and of what motivates them.

Moral development

An interest in pupils as individuals is clearly necessary here, but on its own is not sufficient. Any discussion of the moral climate of the school also raises questions about discipline, rules and sanctions. Kohlberg (1975) has argued that children's under-standing of right and wrong is related to their level of cognitive development. He proposed six stages of moral development (see Table 5.1), but suggested that many people never progressed beyond stage 4. Kohlberg's higher stages of moral reasoning imply the moral right to question the prevailing norms in a society, as reflected for example in national legislation or in school rules. Thus, rules can, and sometimes should, be challenged.

For teachers, Kohlberg's theory poses an interesting question about the sanction used in schools: To what level of moral reasoning do the most frequently used sanctions appeal? Infant school teachers often rely on appeals to their own relationship with the children, together with insight into the effects of the misbehaviour of other children: 'How do you think Jenny felt when you splashed her work with paint?' This would correspond to stage 3. Similarly, most junior school heads would deal with the occasional case of a child smoking by discussing the harmful and dependency forming effects of the habit, combined, perhaps, with informing the pupil's parents about the incident. This, too,

Table 5.1 **Kohlberg's theory of Moral Reasoning**

Level 1 (Corresponds to Piaget's 'preconventional' stage: approximate age 2–7)

Stage 1 Obedience/conformity due solely to fear of punishment.
Example: You mustn't talk when the teacher tells you to be quiet because you might get told off.

Stage 2 Morality based on 'fair trades'.
Example: You must share your toys with other children so that they will share theirs with you.

Level 2 (Corresponds to Piaget's 'conventional' stage: approximate age 7–11)

Stage 3 Judgement based on desire to please others.
Example: it's wrong to swear because it upsets mum (teacher).

Stage 4 Judgement based on respect for authority, maintaining law and order.
Example: You mustn't break rules even if you don't agree with them. What would happen if everyone decides on rules for themselves?

Level 3 (Corresponds to Piaget's 'post-conventional' stages: age 12 upwards)

Stage 5 Rules can be changed if there is general agreement.
Example: Why is this rule really necessary?

Stage 6 Respect for human dignity: abstract principles can transcend ruled
Example: I won't obey this rule because it's against my principles.

---

could correspond to stage 3. In secondary schools rules are sometimes more explicit, sometimes with a 'tariff' system: 'If you forget your games kit you get a detention', or 'if you are caught fighting you run round the field five times in the lunch hour'. Tariff systems of this kind appeal to the lowest level of moral reasoning, and are really more appropriate for pre-school children. They are, of course, economical in the teacher's time. Moreover they can have a deterrent value in persuading other pupils as well as the pupil concerned, not to commit the same offence again. Yet from the point of view of personal and social development they are at best useless. They do nothing to develop understanding of the moral legitimacy of rules, nor, incidentally, do they give teachers any incentive for questioning the necessity for a rule. Rather they encourage deviousness by instilling respect for the eleventh commandment: 'Thou shalt not be found out'.

Finding more constructive alternatives is not impossible, but does require time, imagination and a genuine concern for the pupil's welfare. In one school teachers were seeking the culprits responsible for a particularly offensive piece of graffiti. Perhaps feeling that the investigation was likely to succeed, two girls 'owned up' to the offence and proposed a 'punishment'. They would clean the offending walls in their own time, design a mural to replace their graffiti, buy the necessary materials and paint the design, which would first have been approved by the deputy head. This would cost them money, and a good deal of time.

Hearing this story, some teachers argue indignantly that accepting this offer would be 'giving in' to the girls, and would not be a proper punishment because they would enjoy both the activity and the attention associated with it. In fact, the girls' proposal was accepted. The moral climate of the school aimed to help pupils accept responsibility for their own actions. A more conventionally punitive response would have further antagonised pupils who were already disaffected. The outcome of this particular offence enabled the pupils to contribute something useful to the school, and provided an opportunity to raise their self-esteem rather than lower it.

A further, and encouraging, implication of Kohlberg's work is that teachers are able to raise the level of their pupils' moral reasoning. In other words, this is not solely related to their level of cognitive development. A series of studies has shown that pupils' moral reasoning level is raised by discussing moral dilemmas with peers who have a higher level of moral reasoning ability (e.g. Blatt and Kohlberg, 1973). Hence, providing an opportunity for discussion of controversial issues may raise pupils' level of moral awareness. It does not, of course, follow that their behaviour will improve, and this lack of any necessary relationship between moral reasoning ability and actual behaviour is a major limitation in Kohlberg's work. Nevertheless, developing the ability to think analytically about questions of moral judgement does provide a basis for choice in real life, especially if conclusions reached in class discussion are consistent with the moral climate prevailing in the school.

What we are arguing here is that an objective for pupils' cognitive and moral development is to help them take increasing responsibility for their own behaviour. There is indirect evidence for the benefits of this from other sources. In their study of 12 London secondary schools, Rutter *et al* (1979) noted that the more effective schools tended to involve pupils in decisions about the running of the school, for example, by means of a pupil council. Reynolds (1976) reached a similar conclusion when he noted that the more successful Welsh secondary modern schools in his sample had a prefect system in which older pupils had responsibility for certain aspects of the behaviour of others.

Conclusions

We have argued in this chapter that teachers have responsibilities for their pupils' welfare which extend beyond responsibility for their educational progress. It is a fallacy, though, to regard welfare responsibilities as an obstacle to effective class-room teaching. This is because effective teaching requires a 'moral climate' in the classroom which facilitates communication within the class on matters relevant to the children's welfare outside it. School can provide the element of stability, experience of success and the chance of a secure relationship with an adult which enables some pupils to cope with the stress they experience at home. On the other hand school can also be an additional source of stress for some pupils. In such cases it is all too easy for professionals to attribute the pupil's problems solely to the home, ignoring the compounding effect of negative experiences at school. Yet the more effective teachers are in the classroom, the more likely it becomes that they will need on occasions to find time to talk to pupils and their parents individually. This raises a very different set of questions, to which we turn in the next chapter.

Questions and exercises

1. Look for an opportunity to 'shadow' a pupil or group of pupils for one day. What do you observe about the pupils' behaviour and attitude in different classes/situations?
2. Make a list of references to family life in school assembly over a 2 week period. What model of family life is provided? Carry out the same exercise looking at classroom and corridor displays, and/or at reading books used by younger pupils.
3. Which pupils in your class have acquired a reputation, for example for arriving late to lessons, or for asking 'silly' questions? How does your response help them to shed this reputation? Alternatively, how does your response strengthen it?
4. With a group of colleagues, make a list of 6–10 emotional needs of pupils you teach. *Independently*, put them in a rank order of importance. Then discuss the differences in the rank orders. What does this tell you about your own values and priorities?

Recommended reading

Galloway, D. (1981) *Teaching and Counselling: Pastoral Care in Primary and Secondary Schools*. London, Longman.
Hargreaves, D. H., Hestor, S. K. and Mellor, F. J. (1975) *Deviance in Classrooms*. London, Routledge and Kegan Paul.
Pring, R. (1984) *Personal and Social Education in the Curriculum*. London, Hodder and Stoughton.
White, J. (1982) *The Aims of Education Restated*. London, Routledge.

CHAPTER 6

Talking with individuals

Introduction

All teachers have to talk with pupils and with their parents on an individual basis from time to time. Quite apart from routine parents evenings, either teachers or parents may want to discuss some aspect of a child's progress or behaviour. In addition, teachers often want to follow up incidents that occur in the course of the day's work in the classroom on a one-to-one basis. Such interviews may be formal, in the sense that either teacher or parent has requested them. In the infant years they are at least as likely to be informal, with a parent or teacher asking for a quick chat at the beginning or end of school. This can be irritating when the request comes from a parent at a time when the teacher is busily preparing the day's work or tidying up, but most infant teachers recognise the value of such informal contacts for both parties.

Regrettably, as children grow older, informal contact of this sort with parents becomes more difficult to achieve. With pupils, though, it remains the norm. In secondary schools pastoral care staff may set aside 20 minutes or more to talk to a particular pupil, but most individual contacts arise spontaneously as the occasion demands.

It is probably not helpful to debate whether such contacts, however they arise, are counselling interviews. Counselling involves a helping relationship in which a counsellor works with a client to clarify the nature of a problem experienced or presented by a client, and to explore possible solutions (p. 4). In one sense, this definition would include almost all contacts between teachers and pupils, or between teachers and parents. On the other hand in counselling the problem is generally regarded as the principal focus, whereas in contacts between teachers and pupils or parents the principal focus is the child's progress and adjustment at school.

At one level this distinction is not very convincing, since counselling interviews carried out by a trained counsellor, social worker or educational psychologist may also have a wider aim than overcoming a specific problem. Nevertheless, there are dangers in teachers regarding themselves as counsellors. The most valuable experience teachers can give a pupil is an active sense of belonging to the class and to the wider school community. The role of counsellor/therapist to an individual pupil is not incompatible with this, but teachers' responsibility to the whole class can conflict with their wish to help individuals. Hence, there is a risk of creating role confusion, both for pupils and for teachers.

It may even be unhelpful to regard the majority of one-to-one contacts between teachers and pupils as 'interviews', let alone 'counselling interviews'. An interview implies a power relationship between interviewer and interviewee. It also implies a degree of formality. There undoubtedly is a power relationship between teachers and pupils, and this is often evident to both parties, for example in discipline situations. On the other hand, many contacts take place informally in circumstances in which the teacher is consciously wanting not to emphasise his or her position as an adult or teacher. On such occasions talking with a parent or pupil could be a more accurate description of what the teacher is intending than interviewing them. Whether it is perceived in the same way by the pupil or parent is, however, open to question.

Purpose of interviews

The purpose of individual contacts with pupil and parents may be influenced by the teacher's effectiveness in the classroom. Less effective teachers are likely to find themselves involved more frequently in disciplinary interviews about behavioural problems, either with children or with their parents. They may also find they have more requests for interviews from parents worried about their children's progress. In contrast, more effective teachers are likely to have greater awareness of children's personal needs, and may be more sensitive to children's own attempts to seek help or advice. In addition, parents who are not worried about their child's progress at school may find it easier to approach teachers for advice on problems they are experiencing at home than parents who feel dissatisfied with the school.

However, a word of caution is needed here. Neither children nor parents nor, for that matter, teachers find it easy to talk about personally sensitive issues. Children who tell a teacher they have been sexually abused at home seldom request an interview and come straight to the point. Rather they may start talking about something quite different, and the real problem only emerges in the course of patient discussion. Similarly, parents may start by asking about their child's progress or behaviour at school, and it will only gradually emerge that they have sought an interview because of their concern about their child's behaviour at home. That said, most contacts do *not* have this 'indirect' purpose. We should only assume that there may be some 'deeper' significance if the client is obviously not satisfied by the initial discussion.

Scope of chapter

However we think about individual contacts with pupils or parents, they require some of the skills needed by counsellors. Thus, we shall look briefly at some of the skills needed in interviewing, and argue that these should be seen as building on skills which are integral to effective teaching. We shall also look briefly at the complex issue of non-verbal communication in interviewing, and again argue that awareness of the issues involved is equally important in the classroom. Disciplinary interviews need to be discussed in their own right, if only because they occur so frequently, and the same applies to interviews which focus explicitly on the pupil's curriculum. Finally, we look at the special questions that arise when talking with children under severe stress.

Interviewing skills

In the last 15 years the literature on interviewing skills has mushroomed. Much of it has been aimed at counsellors and others in the helping professions. Yet with a few exceptions such as Ann Jones' (1984) excellent book for secondary teachers, much of this literature is of limited value to class teachers. The emphasis on interviewing skills draws on a different theoretical and philosophical tradition to teaching. For this reason it can be intimidating, implying the need to acquire a new set of skills, over and above the 'craft of the classroom' (Marland, 1975). We shall look here at 4 stages in any discussion or interview, and argue that this is not the case.

Opening gambits

Students are taught at an early stage in their initial teacher education courses not to start classroom discussions with a 'closed' question. Whether they learn not to do so is, of course, more questionable. The theory, though, is uncontroversial. The same principle applies in talking with pupils or parents on a one-to-one basis.

How to open a discussion must naturally depend on its purpose and who sought the meeting. Nevertheless, it is important to recognise that the problem may appear in a totally different light to the various parties involved. Thus, for the teacher the problem may be the pupil's repeated lateness to school in the morning. The explanation may be straightforward, involving easily avoidable delay when walking to school, or the need to drop a younger brother off at the primary school on the way. Occasionally, though, the explanation may be more complex, perhaps involving the child in arriving late to avoid bullying in the playground or on the way to school. In such cases it is naive for two reasons to expect the child willingly to tell the teacher what is happening. First, the pupil recognises he is in trouble, and hence that the teacher is angry. Seeking sympathy from an authority figure with whom you are in trouble is much harder than it sounds. Second, the child may well have been threatened with punitive action from other pupils if she 'snitches' to the teacher. In such circumstances the direct question 'Why were you late?' is likely to elicit an evasive 'don't know' or an untruthful but socially acceptable 'I got up too late'. The even more direct question: 'What time did you leave home?' provides an even easier escape route. Hence, just as a successful classroom discussion starts with a question that leaves open a number of avenues for the children to explore, the same principle applies in individual discussions.

In the same way, when parents have requested a meeting, it is important to give *them* a chance to talk. At all levels, from nursery school to university, teachers tend to talk too much. Learning to listen to pupils is a necessary skill in the classroom. It is just as necessary in individual interviews, either with pupils or with parents. The nature of the relationship implies that the 'client' may start the discussion feeling anxious, tense or resentful. In such circumstances, patience is needed to avoid closing the discussion prematurely, and thus losing the opportunity to help.

Clarifying the nature of the problem

Recent research in effective teaching has been concerned with 'metacognition', or the child's ability to monitor what is happening and respond appropriately. Nisbet and Schucksmith (1986) suggest that the extent to which children 'learn to learn' is a key factor. They argue that effective teachers teach pupils how to monitor what they are doing, so they become skilled at working out solutions for themselves. There is a parallel here with interviewing.

In the classroom, a teacher will aim to help children see for themselves where they have gone wrong, or what they need to do next when working on a project. The solution, or next stage, then becomes a matter for agreement between pupil and teacher. Time constraints may make this difficult if not impossible, but the aim remains valid. Similarly, in an individual interview the aim is to arrive at an agreed definition of the nature of the problem. This will only be likely if the teacher is able to keep an open mind as the discussion progresses. Keeping an open mind implies the need to monitor the interview as it progresses, with an attempt to recognise the pupil's or parent's feelings. At times the teacher will need to use what the counselling literature calls 'reflecting back'. This has the effect of encouraging clients to develop a particular issue without defining it for them. Examples are: 'You say you met these older boys on your way to school', or 'You say Peter has seemed anxious at home recently'. Once again, we come back to the skills of accurate listening and keeping an open mind as to the outcome of the discussion.

Guidance or Advice?

An aim of personal and social education is to help pupils increasingly to accept responsibility for their own actions and decisions. Similarly, in other areas of the primary and secondary curriculum teachers try to show pupils how to find solutions for themselves rather than tell them the answer. This involves the skills of metacognition we discussed above. In some circumstances, though, straightforward, clear information is needed. This applies in the classroom and in individual interviews. It is not hard to think of examples in the classroom, but they occur less frequently when talking with individuals. Sometimes a child will need factual information, for example regarding the normality of some aspect of puberty. Again, parents sometimes need factual information on welfare entitlements, for example regarding uniform allowances.

There is a useful distinction, though, between giving information the person has requested, giving advice and offering guidance. Information is often needed in order to make an informed decision. Giving advice implies that *we* think the people we are talking to should follow a particular course of action. Guidance implies a possible course of action which may be arrived at jointly, thus retaining the client's sense of responsibility and involvement.

It is often flattering to be asked for advice. Indeed, as an educational psychologist I found that coaching a pupil to seek advice from a teacher was often the quickest and most effective way to change a teacher's negative attitude towards the pupil. It sometimes changed the pupil's attitude to the teacher too. Nevertheless, giving advice carries risks.

If we respond directly to a request for advice we put the people with whom we are talking in a dependent position. If we offer unsolicited advice, we put them in a defensive position. Neither dependency nor defensiveness offer a sound basis from which to make up one's own mind. Nevertheless, by the end of the interview both parties should feel that something useful has been achieved. This, too, has parallels with the ordinary work of the classroom.

Closing interviews

Finishing a lesson is another of the skills all teachers have to learn. Often this involves a summing up of what has been covered. Pupils leave the classroom feeling they have achieved something, and ready to continue on the next occasion from where they left off. The same principle applies in interviewing. From the client's point of view, it is the teacher's responsibility not to let the discussion carry on for too long, just as pupils expect the teacher to start *and* finish lessons promptly. Again, clients have an expectation that the meeting should have some obvious purpose, even if this has been mainly for the teacher's benefit. They also need to know if and when further meetings will take place.

When talking about closing interviews, it is worth adding two qualifications. First, some interviews should be postponed right from the start. Pupils may ask to talk to a teacher at a time when the teacher is busy. It is much better not to start a discussion in such circumstances, but to ask them to come back at a specified time later when you will be able to give them more time. Second, an important interviewing skill is knowing the limits to one's own competence. It is sometimes necessary to tell pupils or parents when they seek guidance that you do not think you are the person who can best help them. It then becomes possible to discuss whether a senior colleague, or a member of one of the support services may be the most appropriate person.

Verbal and non-verbal communication

Teachers, like everyone else, are the product of their own cultural backgrounds. Each culture develops its own conventions, both in speech and in non-verbal communication. These conventions may not be understood by members of other groups. This is not simply a question of awareness of ethnic differences, though these are important. Misunderstanding can also occur between people from different geographical areas and different social backgrounds. Differences in the meaning attached to the same word provide amusing examples. 'Got a fag, mate?' can mean 'Can you give me a cigarette?' in London and 'Could you take me to a homosexual?' in New York. On moving to Sheffield from London I was at first disconcerted to hear burly, steel workers calling each other 'love', and even more disconcerted when they called me 'love'. What is a term of endearment used within the family in one sub-culture may be a term of familiarity between women in another and between any two people talking to each other in a third.

It is easy to underestimate the importance of cultural differences. They often lead to serious misunderstandings both in the classroom and when teachers talk to pupils and parents on an individual basis. Ironically, although they purport to be concerned with interpersonal relationships, many counselling texts are appallingly ethnocentric. By this we mean that they give the impression that cultural differences are either irrelevant or non-existent. Thus, the first edition of a widely used 'cookbook' of counselling skills (Munro *et al* 1979) totally ignores cultural differences, although intended initially for use in New Zealand, a country where cross-cultural communication is a topical issue. Again, Liberman *et al* (1975) blandly assure us that: 'eye contact is almost always the *sine qua non* for personal effectiveness'. At best such statements are grossly misleading, leading to confusion and resentment. Eye contact, in fact, illustrates the point very well.

Many teachers may regard a pupil who cannot or will not make eye contact as devious or unreliable. This is particularly true in disciplinary situations. Yet in some cultures, for a child to make eye contact in such circumstances would be the height of insolence. It is not simply a question of *how* eye contact is made. Certainly, pupils *can* look insolently at teachers, and sometimes do. The point, though, is that *any* eye contact between a child and an adult in authority would be considered bad manners in some cultures. It is thus unfortunate that a child's conscious attempts to be polite may increase the teacher's ire. Non-verbal messages that are readily understood within a culture frequently cause confusion between cultures. Raised eye-brows, for example, is generally taken to imply a request for more explanation: 'I haven't understood you'. Amongst Maori and Polynesian people in New Zealand it implies the opposite: 'Yes, I have understood you'. A shrug of the shoulders is often taken to mean: 'I don't care', and as such is particularly irritating to teachers. In some cultures it means: 'I don't know'.

Aspects of non-verbal communication

In a useful review of non-verbal communication in counselling interviews between people of different cultures, Vogelaar and Silverman (1984) identify three principal categories of non-verbal behaviour. The first includes all gestures, facial expressions, cultural conventions on eye contact and posture. The last is quite frequently a source of tension. Many counselling texts from America advocate, often in a very didactic way, that the interviewer should show concern by leaning forward in her chair. However, this is likely to be misunderstood in many parts of Britain as over-familiarity.

The second category of non-verbal communication raises a similar problem. This refers to the use and perception of social and personal space. If a person sits or stands too close we feel uncomfortable. It is an intrusion into our personal space. In disciplinary interviews teachers sometimes deliberately stand close to pupils as a way of dominating them. There are interesting status and social class differences here, with a tendency for higher status people to expect greater social distance in conversation and other social encounters. Again, it is worth noting that many counselling texts published in North America advocate that the counsellor sits much closer to the client than would be regarded as normal in Britain. Indeed, any teacher in England who followed the instructions in such texts would be considered to be behaving intrusively.

The third group of non-verbal behaviour refers to *how* something is said as opposed to *what* is said. In other words, it includes all the vocal cues we use in recognising the feelings which lie behind what the other person is saying. Once again, the scope for misunderstanding is almost unlimited. The stereotypes of the stiff-upper-lip Englishman and the dour Scot may be caricatures, but they do illustrate how expression of emotion is culturally based. Even in schools with few children from minority ethnic groups, teachers frequently have little first-hand knowledge of their pupils' cultural background. A sensitive awareness of differences in cultural conventions in verbal and non-verbal behaviour is important in the classroom as well as in individual discussions with pupils and their parents.

Disciplinary interviews

Discipline is probably the most frequent reason for teachers seeing a pupil individually. In many primary schools it is still quite common practice for pupils to be sent to see the headteacher when they misbehave. In many secondary schools they are sent to the head of department or, more often, the head of year. The use of senior staff in this way is controversial. There is a strong argument that it undermines the authority of the referring teacher by implying that only a more senior member of staff can deal with the problem. Nevertheless it remains true that senior staff frequently find themselves following up incidents of unacceptable behaviour, as do class teachers in primary and form tutors in secondary schools. We are concerned here with the purpose of such interviews, the possible 'hidden' messages they may convey, and the way pupils may interpret them.

Conflicting perceptions?

It is easy to avoid thinking clearly about what we are trying to achieve when talking to pupils about incidents of unacceptable behaviour. Legitimate aims include establishing the facts, trying to persuade the pupil to see why the behaviour is unacceptable, deciding whether punishment is appropriate, and if so what form it should take, finding out whether the pupil is affected by other factors such as a clash with a particular teacher, difficulty with a particular subject, bullying at school or friction within the family. The problem lies partly in the potential blurring of the distinction between discipline and counselling and partly in the potential lack of clarity in the pupil's eyes regarding the purpose of the interview and its outcome.

The distinction between a disciplinary interview and a counselling one is not always as straightforward as it may seem at first sight. When pupils are frequently in trouble, there is a natural tendency for a teacher to try to break the cycle. This may involve a conscious attempt to show them that teachers are interested in them as individuals and sympathetic to any problems they may be experiencing at school or at home. From the pupil's point of view, though, this can seem like prying. Moreover, looking for 'deeper' reasons for disruptive behaviour implicitly denies pupils responsibility for their own actions. As one 14-year-old said: 'What I did were wrong and he should have punished me for it but he didn't have any right to go asking about my family.'

A gender issue is related to this. Dweck *et al* (1978) found a tendency for teachers to attribute boys' misbehaviour to factors which they could themselves control, and for which they should be punished. In contrast, there was a tendency to attribute girls' misbehaviour to emotional or psychological problems which would require a more sympathetic counselling approach. The implication is that girls are less likely than boys to be held accountable for their own actions, a conclusion which few people would wish to defend.

Nevertheless it remains part of the class teacher's or form tutor's job to try to establish the reason for common problems. The behaviourist view that analysis of classroom interaction is the key to behaviour change is at best simplistic. The reason is that analysis of interaction within the classroom tells us nothing about the relevance of problems outside the classroom (Berger, 1982). Yet from the pupil's perspective it remains important to distinguish clearly between the disciplinary and counselling aspects when talking to pupils individually. The same applies in interviews with parents. It is one thing to ask parents to visit the school in order to enlist their support in requiring their children to behave acceptably and warn them of the consequences if they do not. It is quite another to ask them to visit the school in order to seek their advice on reasons for their children's problems and to discuss with them how the school may most effectively respond. Either reason for inviting parents to the school is legitimate, though the second is more constructive. Confusing the two, however, is a recipe for confusion and resentment.

Work-related interviews

Each year a massive amount of formal testing takes place in schools. With the introduction of the national curriculum, attainment targets and national testing at 7, 11, 14 and 16, this seems likely to increase. Educational research foundations depend heavily on the royalties from sales of tests to remain solvent. Many of the tests claim to be diagnostic, and to enable the teacher to plan future work for the pupil. It is therefore surprising how little educational use is made of the results. They appear almost to constitute displacement activities – a term used in animal ethology to describe actions that appear irrelevant to any threat to the animal but which have the effect of reducing its anxiety level.

Brief discussion with children individually to talk about their work are among the most effective ways of giving them a sense of involvement and responsibility for their work. Discussing the results of diagnostic testing can reduce the sense of helplessness which is so often felt by children with learning difficulties. The problem of time is a familiar one but does not always stand close scrutiny. Opportunities can be found in registration or in quiet moments when the class is working on a set task to talk to pupils individually. Indeed, it is difficult to see how to justify spending time on a testing programme, let alone on diagnostic testing, if we do not find time to discuss the results and their implications with children.

In secondary schools the rapid growth of modular courses in the fourth and fifth year, together with the introduction of records of achievement provide further scope for involving pupils in educational decisions that affect them. Many records of achievement require an assessment from pupils themselves, thus providing a focus for one-to-one discussion with pupils. Unfortunately, some schools have yet to think constructively about how this may be achieved. The role of the form tutor is increasingly being recognised as crucial; the organisation and time tabling of tutorial work can create opportunities for tutors to talk about curriculum choices with individuals or groups – or make it virtually impossible for them to do so.

Children under stress

A minority of pupils live in home circumstances that by any standards would be acutely stressful. Teachers are better placed than most people to recognise the effect of adverse home conditions and sometimes feel indignant at the reluctance of social workers to take steps to remove children from them. For their part, social workers recognise the limitations in what can be offered if the child comes into care.

Children's resilience is often under-estimated. As Rutter (1978, 1981) points out they can usually cope with single isolated sources of stress, however severe, if they really are isolated. Unfortunately sources of stress are *not* always isolated. It is one thing to cope with your parents' arguments. It is quite another to cope with this *and* one parent's psychiatric illness, *and* chronic financial and housing problems *and* the terminal illness of a grandparent living at home. School plays a critical role. It can be a source of stability where you feel accepted and where your achievements, as well as difficulties, are recognised. Alternatively it can be, as Hargreaves (1982) suggests, a place where your self-esteem is lowered still further, and where the only thing that is raised is your sense of inadequacy and helplessness.

For teachers, the message is clear: the more severe the stress the pupil experiences at home, the more important is the support that comes from active involvement in the curriculum and social life of the school. We seldom serve pupils living in disadvantaged or stressful homes well by reducing our expectations of them.

This said, the pastoral element in teachers' work inevitably gives them access to confidential information about pupils' lives. It can also give them responsibilities in situations which they themselves may find stressful. We shall look briefly at three of these after considering the problem of confidentiality.

Confidentiality

It is tempting to give pupils or parents an assurance that anything they say to us privately will be held in the strictest confidence. Teachers have neither a legal nor a moral justification, however, in giving absolute assurances on confidentiality. The law does not accept the right of teachers to withhold information they regard as privileged. Technically, any records kept by teachers are the property of the employing LEA. Further, if a teacher is told anything that implies danger to the life or health of another person, confidentiality cannot be maintained. An example might be if the children's mother told a teacher that her husband was physically or sexually abusing them. In such cases the teacher's responsibilities have recently been clarified in a circular from the DES (1988c).

Child abuse

This term includes emotional and physical neglect as well as physical or sexual ill-treatment (DHSS, 1988). The DES Circular recommends LEAs to designate a senior official as having responsibility for co-ordinating policy throughout the LEA. It recommends each school to nominate a senior member of staff for co-ordinating action within the school, and for liaising with other agencies in accordance with the LEA's procedures. The principal responsibility for protecting children from abuse rests with the local Social Services Department, though both the Police and the NSPCC also have statutory responsibilities.

The signs of child abuse are seldom unambiguous. Outward evidence such as burns, bruises or cuts are less frequent than the less obvious evidence of neglect. This includes poor clothing, hunger, unusually slow growth, and excessively attention-seeking or dependent behaviour. Signs of sexual abuse are even less obvious but may include precocity in sexual talk, or withdrawn behaviour. None of these are firm evidence that abuse has occurred, but because they work more closely with children than any other professionals, teachers are in a uniquely favourable position to observe any evidence that suggests it may be taking place. If teachers suspect child abuse, they should inform the senior teacher with co-ordinating responsibility in the area, who should then follow the LEA's procedure. These will include contacting named officers of the Education Department and of the Social Services Department.

Bereavement

A century ago all moderately experienced teachers would have had first hand experience of pupils dying as well as pupils' parents. Today this is no longer the case, and the death of a pupil, or a pupil's friend or relative is a much less frequent occurrence than formerly. Even less frequent, and perhaps even more disturbing is the case of a child with a terminal illness. Lansdown (1980) suggests that such children should live in as normal an environment as possible, preferably attending an ordinary rather than a special school. He argues:

Children expect to go to school, no matter how much they may complain. What is more, if they are going to die at twelve then school life will have been virtually their whole life, so it is doubly important to ensure that it is of the highest possible quality.
(p 155)

Teachers do not always recognise how much they can do to help their pupils, and parents, cope with their loss in a positive way. Unfortunately, teachers can also contribute to the emotional damage that can result from the tendency in Anglo-Saxon culture to suppress talk about death, implicitly denying its finality. It is helpful to recognise common reactions in families following bereavement. These include shock or numbness, feelings of guilt, general apathy and even preoccupation with the dead child's image, 'seeing' or 'hearing' her or him in the house (Burton, 1974; Lansdown, 1980).

Teachers often ask whether children should attend the funerals of friends or relatives. The consensus view is that they should be encouraged to attend. Parents sometimes feel 'he's not old enough to understand it'. This is understandable, but almost always mistaken. The child will certainly be old enough to understand that something that affects her *and* her family is being kept from her. When calling or telephoning to express sympathy, teachers are in a good position to suggest gently that, of course, Jimmy will be away from school for the funeral. When a child dies, it is often appreciated by parents if his or her friends come to the funeral with their teacher (see Goldacre, 1978 for a particularly sensitive discussion of this).

Teachers can also help by unobtrusively creating opportunities for a child to talk about a lost relative, or for the rest of the class to talk about their classmate who has died. In the latter case, it is helpful to keep some of the child's work on the wall displays. Also, maintaining contact with the school can be helpful to parents, indicating not only that their child is remembered but also that they themselves are remembered. The expression of grief is important to its resolution. The psychological problems for children or adults that sometimes follow bereavement are usually associated with inability to express grief. When adults say of a child: 'He got over it so well; never cried at all' this is almost invariably an indication that the child has *not* started to cope with his loss. Thus, as well as playing a low-key part in helping children and parents to cope with bereavement, teachers are in a good position to note the occasions when professional help may be needed.

Separation and divorce

There are few classes in which some children have not experienced the trauma of their parents' separation or divorce. There is clear evidence that this is associated with an increased risk of anti-social behaviour for boys, though girls are less likely to react in this way (e.g. Rutter *et al*, 1970). It is worth emphasising that their parents separating may be a less harmful alternative for some children than their remaining together in a feuding or abusive relationship. On the other hand, the consequences of separation can be prolonged. A change of house or school may be necessary; there may be acute financial problems; the child may be the centre of a custody dispute, encouraged to 'take sides' against one parent; a parent may develop minor but disturbing psychiatric problems such as depression, and so on. Separation, in other words, may be associated with a change in life-style so profound that parents and children feel that their previous sense of identity is threatened.

What then is the teacher's role? There are three central points. First, they must be clear about which parent has custody, and about the other parent's rights of access to the child. There have been incidents of children being abducted from school by a parent who has been denied access by the courts. However, this quasi-legal responsibility is distinct from the need to remain impartial in what is essentially a family dispute. This can be difficult since parents who are themselves in an upset or angry state can make determined efforts to involve others, including teachers, in their argument.

Second, when children are under immense stress at home, teachers can help in small but important ways at school. Financial problems may make it impossible for a parent to provide the full school uniform. Conditions in the home may be hopelessly unsuitable for homework. Following a change of address transport to school may be difficult. At such times understanding and flexibility from the school can be all important.

Third, children are often relieved to know that their teacher knows what has happened, or is happening. All too often, children are caught up in a conflict which they do not fully understand and which, they feel, they cannot talk about with anyone outside the family. It is this sense of secrecy, as much as the fact of separation, which can be damaging. With few exceptions, children can cope with the truth however stressful; they find it much harder to cope with their fantasies about things that are left to their imagination. This is how some children come to feel responsible for their parents' separation, believing that had it not been for them their parents would still be together.

The teacher's task is to give all children an opportunity to talk about what is happening at home. The chance to talk to someone who is not caught up in the unhappiness and anger of the home can help children to sort out their own feelings about it. Some teachers fill this sort of counselling role very effectively. Others feel distinctly uncomfortable, and should probably not attempt it. We should not, however, underestimate the school's potential for supporting children in times of family crisis. As an educational psychologist I frequently saw pupils who had been referred to the service because of their difficult behaviour at school. Surprisingly often, a meeting with the child and a parent revealed family upheavals of which the teacher was unaware. With very few exceptions indeed, the children were eager for a liked and respected teacher to know about these. The fact that they were no longer 'on their own' was itself a potent source of support.

Conclusions

We have argued in this chapter that face-to-face interviews with pupils or parents require many of the same skills as classroom teaching. The undoubted necessity for individual discussion should not obscure the point that the teacher's *principal* responsibility is for the child's educational welfare, and most individual interviews will have this in mind. That said, there are occasions when teachers have the opportunity to provide an important source of support for stress the child is experiencing at home. Throughout the chapter we have made numerous references to discussions with parents. This is such an important topic that it deserves a chapter in its own right.

Questions and exercises

1. Clare is very quiet in the classroom. You really don't feel you know her. She is often shabbily dressed. A dinner lady says her father has a record of violence, but hasn't provided more details. Her parents don't turn up for open evenings. Write a short letter inviting her parents to visit the school. Discuss the letters you write within the group. Will they achieve the desired result?
2. Clare's parents *do* turn up. Role play the interview with her class teacher. If possible video this and discuss it.
3. What cultural differences in *non-verbal* behaviour can you observe between children in your present school, *or* between these children and children in other schools you know?
4. What arrangements has your school made for dealing with suspected child abuse?
5. What regular testing is carried out in your school? How could you use the results to involve children more actively in their work?

6. Thinking of pupils whose parents have recently separated, what support *has* the school provided? What support do you think it might have been able to provide?
7. Ask yourself the same questions in relation to a pupil who has suffered a recent bereavement.

Recommended reading

Lansdown, R. (1980) *More than Sympathy*. London, Tavistock.

Jones, A. (1984) *Counselling Adolescents: School and After*. London, Kogan Page.

Maher, P. (1987) *Child Abuse: The Educational Perspective*. Oxford, Blackwell.

Nelson-Jones, R. (1986) *Human Relationship Skills*. Eastbourne, Holt, Rinehart and Winston.

Vogelaar, L. M. E. and Silverman, M. S. (1984) Non-verbal Communication in Cross Cultural Counselling: A Literature Review. *International Journal for the Advancement of Counselling*, 7, 41–57.

CHAPTER 7

Bringing parents in

Introduction

All schools claim to welcome parents. Indeed, it appears an almost compulsory part of the rhetoric of school prospectuses that parents are welcome. Many go further and talk of parents as 'partners' with teachers in their children's education, perhaps influenced by the Warnock Report on Special Educational Needs (DES, 1978) which devoted a chapter to the concept of partnership. Yet there are few areas in which the gap between rhetoric and reality is greater. Partnership implies the willingness and ability of each party to learn from the other. That implies teachers' willingness and ability to talk as equals with parents whom they may consider responsible for their children's problems, accepting that these parents may have valuable advice to offer on their children's management and motivation.

That the Warnock Report's chapter on partnership *was* rhetoric is evident from Warnock's subsequent observations. In her much-quoted Dimbleby lecture in 1985 she argued that the emphasis on partnership had been exaggerated, since:

> In educational matters, parents cannot be the equal of teachers if teachers are to be regarded as true professionals. Even though educating a child is a joint enterprise, involving both home and school, parents should realise that they cannot have the last word. It is a question of collaboration, not partnership. Sometimes it must be acknowledged that the teacher knows best. (p. 12)

Warnock acknowledged teacher stereotypes of parents: the 'pushy' and the 'indifferent', but did not seriously tackle the problem that at times, both in educational and in family matters, parents might know a great deal more about their child than teachers.

Schools in Britain compare unfavourably with those in the EEC countries in terms of the quality of cooperation between home and school (Macbeth, 1984). A deeply entrenched part of staff-room folklore in many schools, especially those serving council housing estates, inner-city areas and areas with many pupils from minority ethnic communities is that parental 'apathy' is widespread. Yet the same parents whom teachers dismiss as apathetic also find themselves expected to achieve the near-impossible. Marland (1985) quotes research by Johnson and Ransom (1983) that parents felt themselves being scrutinised by teachers on open-evenings and held accountable for their children's progress. Marland continues:

Indeed, sometimes parents' evenings are virtually a handbook, in which the teacher says in effect: "We professionals who've been trained can't handle your son. Could you please, over the next weekend change him so that we can cope more easily". It is like saying: 'I've failed, now you do it – by remote control'! (p. 96)

A one-sidedness is evident in many schools' 'liaison' with parents. Johnson and Ranson (1983) identified this in a survey which showed clearly that teachers saw their task as educating parents about the school, rather than as understanding the parents' own values and priorities. Co-operative parents, then, are parents who don't rock the boat, content to support the school even when a more objective view might suggest that the child's curricula or social needs are being met inadequately.

The evidence does not support the stereotype of parental apathy. Numerous studies of parental interest in their children's education have demonstrated that parents are far more actively involved than is accepted by the conventional wisdom of many staff-rooms (e.g. Johnson and Ranson, 1983).

In the rest of this chapter we shall consider how teachers may make schools more 'parent-friendly' places, and look at the ways teachers and form tutors may contribute to this. First, though, we need to review the impact of recent legislation on the relationship between teachers and their pupils' parents.

Recent legislation and its impact on teacher-parent relationships

Background

The 1944 Education Act held teachers as *in loco parentis* while children were in their care. Subsequent legislation has not altered this, but has greatly modified it. To understand the background to this, we need to look briefly at the present government's analysis of the ills of the education system. In summary, its argument is:

(a) that teachers, encouraged by radical councils, have used their control of the curriculum to peddle subversive left-wing ideologies against the wishes of a majority of parents;

(b) that teachers have consistently shown themselves to be more concerned with their conditions of service and with their control of the curriculum than with evaluating the curriculum in the light of the changing needs of the country;

(c) that the curriculum is unsuited to a large minority of pupils, and that this, together with the former GCE/CSE examination led to widespread under-achievement for which teachers refused to accept accountability, preferring instead to blame parents or the government;
(d) that teachers have either prevented or discouraged necessary involvement in schools by parents, the local community and industry.

I am not concerned here with the validity or otherwise of these charges, except to note that the paranoid fantasy of left-wing ideologues controlling the curriculum is one which arouses baffled bemusement in the overwhelming majority of staff-rooms. We must, however, be concerned with the government's solutions to the alleged problems. In summary again, the solutions have been:

(a) to centralise (or nationalise?) the curriculum;
(b) to weaken the powers of LEA's over the curriculum and over day-to-day administration in schools;
(c) to make teachers more accountable to parents and to their schools' local communities: (i) by increasing parents' rights to choose their children's school; (ii) by requiring schools to publish public examination results; (iii) by imposing conditions of service which required teachers to communicate with parents; (iv) by strengthening the powers of governors and dramatically increasing their responsibilities. The first of these, choice of school, requires a closer look.

Choice of school

The 1980 Education Act greatly reduced the powers of LEAs to control access to schools, and the 1988 Education Reform Act virtually removed them altogether. Lack of space is now the only legitimate reason for refusing a child entry. As important, though, parents now have access to a range of information on which to base a decision. This includes a detailed prospectus, results of public examinations and copies of HMI reports on general inspections. Objectively, this information is hard to interpret. As Gray and Hannon (1986) have convincingly demonstrated, even HMI appear unable to take account of differences between school catchment areas in evaluating their exam results. Moreover, HMI reports are wide open to accidental – or intentional – misinterpretation by the local press. Publication of each school's performance in the national testing programme, as envisaged in the 1988 Education Reform Act, will do nothing to change this situation. Yet although the information available to parents is both incomplete and misleading at an objective level, it is nevertheless having the effect of making schools a great deal more aware of their public image and of their relationships with parents.

Parental involvement in decision-making

Successive Acts have strengthened parents' involvement in decisions affecting their own children, and in decisions about the running of the school in general. The 1980 Education Act gave parents a right of appeal to a local committee when the LEA refused their child access to the school of their choice. If the local committee rules against the parents, they have the right of appeal to the Secretary of State. The 1986 Education Act made provision for similar rights of appeal following exclusion on disciplinary grounds. In the case of children with special educational needs, the 1981 Act gave parents extensive right of involvement in the formal assessment of their children's needs, again with detailed rights of appeal.

This, however, raises an important question about the way professionals interpret the various Acts. In their research on the 1981 Education Act, Goacher *et al* (1988) found that parents were being involved in their children's assessment to the extent that they were kept well informed of the professionals' views. There was much less evidence that parents were actually enabled to contribute to the decisions affecting their children. An obvious interpretation of the evidence is that parents were being 'guided' into accepting provision that already existed in the LEA. Elsewhere I have argued that professionals are under pressure *not* to discuss with parents possibly effective ways of meeting their children's special needs which are not readily available within the LEA (Galloway and Goodwin, 1987).

In all but a small minority of LEAs, the 1986 Education Act strengthened parents' membership of school governing bodies, and the 1988 Act gave them further powers. This will be felt most keenly in two ways. First, governors of all but a minority of smaller primary schools will be responsible for their school's financial management, including the hiring and dismissal of staff. Second, governors are now able to ballot parents as to whether they wish the school to opt out of LEA control by applying to the Secretary of State for grant-maintained status. If 20 per cent of parents ask the governors to hold a ballot, they must do so. If a majority of parents in the ballot vote to opt-out, then the governors must publish proposals for seeking grant maintained status within six months. This will remove the school from the LEA's control altogether, but will also remove it from the support and guidance the LEA may provide.

Information on the curriculum and children's progress

Throughout the 1950s, 1960s and 1970s, the curriculum was known as the 'secret garden' which only teachers might enter. More than in any other country in the world, teachers had the power to decide what was taught, and how. Certainly, their power was constrained by the public examination system and by the inspectorate. Nevertheless, they held the key to the balance between arts and science, and few schools saw the need to make detailed curriculum statements available to parents. It was as though the education system was saying: 'You must send your children to school at the age of five, and you will be liable to prosecution if you don't. But don't expect us to tell you what they should have learned by the time they are seven, let alone whether they *have* actually learned it. All that kind of thing is a matter for our professional judgement. Particularly well-informed middle-class parents could generally get the information they wanted. Others, especially parents of the under-achieving bottom 40 per cent, about whom Sir Keith Joseph so repeatedly expressed concern, felt themselves left, or kept, in the dark.

Joseph encouraged the Manpower Services Commission (MSC) to make substantial sums of money available to schools through the Technical and Vocational Education Initiative. The MSC, however, would only grant money if it approved of the curriculum proposals put forward. This was akin to stealing the key to the professionals' secret garden and trampling on the flower beds. Kenneth Baker went a stage further with his Education Reform Act and ploughed them up.

As a result of the Act schools will be required to follow guidelines laid down in the national curriculum and to teach to attainment targets which children should have reached by the ages of 7, 11, 14 and 16. Further, parents will be told not only whether their children have reached these targets, but also how their school compares with other schools in the LEAs. Again, the additional information parents are given will be difficult, if not impossible, to interpret. Objectively, it may make less difference to what is actually happening in schools then the government would like to believe. Subjectively, though, the Act is likely to exert a profound influence by changing the climate of relationships between schools and parents. Increasingly, schools will have to be sensitive to the aspirations and priorities of their pupils' parents.

It is often argued that making schools more accountable to parental aspirations will result in reduced attention to less able pupils, especially those with special needs. This may be a miscalculation. There has never been a problem of under-achievement in the top 20 per cent of pupils in British schools. Where we may compare unfavourably with our competitor countries in the EEC is in the progress of average and below average pupils, though there is a lack of hard evidence. Schools which favour the minority at the expense of the majority will look unimpressive when test results are published. Schools which consistently neglect the interests of pupils with special needs may find that word quickly filters around the local community.

Making schools parent-friendly

Some hidden messages

Parents won't believe they are welcome just because a prospectus says they are. It could hardly say anything else, could it? They believe what they see and hear for themselves. Or rather, what they come to believe may depend on what they don't see or hear. The process starts before their children's first term at a new school.

Induction

When parents are invited to visit the new school in the Summer term before transfer, the head may tell them a good deal about the school's ethos. They will *learn* a good deal about its ethos from their visit, but not necessarily from what the head says. If the head and selected senior staff do all the talking – and it is disturbing how often prospective parents are expected to sit docilely in the school hall listening to an interminable lecture of unrelieved tedium – they are likely to go away with an impression of hierarchical control in a school which consciously restricts what they see and whom they meet. If, after a brief welcome and state-ment of school policy from the head, they meet their children's future class teacher or form tutor in the classrooms in which they will be taught, they will probably go away with a quite different impression. What you are *not* permitted to see, and the people you do *not* meet can reveal more about a school's climate than what is 'on show'.

The same, incidentally, applies to pupils. They are sceptical about what they hear when teachers from the secondary school visit them in their final year at the primary. They are also scept-ical about what they are told on formal visits. They don't see the places which – for them – are important such as the toilets, nor will they meet the 'tough' teachers about whom kindly older brothers and sisters have warned them. In contrast, the chance to spend a day in the secondary school, being taught by several different teachers, has been shown to be more effective in reducing their anxiety about the new school (Delamont and Gatton, 1986).

Reception areas

Visitors often feel lost on entering a school. Much can be done to create a welcoming impression by posting notices, putting up displays of children's work in a reception area, ensuring that comfortable chairs are available. A welcoming secretary makes a great deal of difference. When teachers visit parents at home they are usually offered a cup of tea or coffee. Reciprocating not only helps to reduce their anxiety, but is a matter of courtesy.

Names and addresses

A simple procedure, understood by all staff, is needed to ensure letters are addressed correctly. This involves more than merely updating addresses. It includes ensuring that letters are not addressed to 'Dear Mr. and Mrs.' in a single-parent family, as well as ensuring that the naming systems of minority ethnic groups are understood. Addressing a letter on the assumption that the parent's or guardian's name is the same as the pupil's can cause embarrassment to everyone concerned, particularly the pupil. Ensuring correct pronunciation of names is also important. Anglicising the pronunciation of names of children from minority ethnic groups is an unintentional indication of lack of respect.

Written communications

Writing letters about routine matters such as school trips or option choices in the fourth year is a skill which does not always come naturally. Letters written in an impersonal bureaucratised form hardly inspire confidence: 'Dear Parents, Please find enclosed herewith . . . . .' Letters written about specific problems can be even more difficult, for example to ask a parent to visit because of concern about the child's behaviour or progress. The critical point here is to convey concern in a way which seeks the parents' help in understanding and solving the problem. Johnson and Ranson (1983) give some excellent examples of effective and ineffective communication.

Access to teachers

A depressingly frequent scenario in secondary schools is of parents being prevented from meeting any teacher who actually knows their child except on open-evening when they are herded from one place to another like stray sheep. Most head teachers would initially deny that this happens, yet it is not unusual for secondary schools to require parents to channel inquiries through the head of year. However reluctant heads of year or even head-teachers may be to acknowledge the fact, parents often prefer to talk to teachers who teach their children on a day-to-day basis, not people who only see them when they are in trouble.

There are, of course, real problems here. Senior staff have more time for interviews with parents than colleagues with a full teaching timetable. In addition, some teachers will lack the expertise to handle potentially difficult interviews. Yet denying parents access to the teachers they are likely to want to meet – the form tutor or teachers of subjects their children are finding difficult – betrays a fundamental lack of trust not only in parents but also in the teachers themselves. One suspects that sometimes colleagues are 'protected' from parents to enable senior members of staff such as heads of year to establish their territory, or sphere of influence, not for the benefit of the colleagues.

A potentially effective way to establish informal contact with parents is through homework diaries on which teachers can write comments or questions, with space for the parents to reply. Whether they are successful depends largely on how much effort teachers put into them. If a signature at the end of each week is all that is expected, parents are likely to regard the diary at best as a tedious chore. If the diary reveals an interest in the child, for example a word of praise for a good, if unsuccessful attempt, it becomes a useful means of communication.

Finding out what parents want

Being clear about what parents expect from the school is not as simple as it sounds. Maureen Stone (1981) has drawn attention to the mismatch between what teachers think parents in ethnic minority groups want and what they actually want: while the school takes pride in the Afro-Caribbean brass band, parents arrange Saturday schooling to compensate for their children's second-rate education, as they see it, on weekdays. A school's musical and sporting tradition can do much to promote its image in the community. They can contribute to pupils' appreciation of the value of cultural diversity. They will not, however, succeed in this if particular groups of pupils are patronisingly perceived as being musical or good at sport but 'not academic'. The hidden curriculum message is that access to the mainstream curriculum, and hence to public examination passes leading to high-status employment, is only for more 'able' pupils from socially privi-leged homes. From here it is a short stop to seeing recognition of musical and sporting achievement as a way of socialising black pupils into acquiescence in a system that denies them success in the school's main activities. At the risk of labouring the point, the argument is simply that encouragement of extra-curricular activities is no substitute for achievement in the mainstream curriculum, not that they lack validity as activities in their own right.

The class teacher's task

How much the individual class or subject teacher can do to foster an effective partnership with parents will depend to some extent on the school's senior management. They can make the school 'parent-friendly', or provide hidden messages that deter parents even more effectively than a printed notice saying: No Parents Beyond this Point. In this section we consider four ways in which class teachers can contribute to the school's overall policy.

Involving parents in the curriculum

Parents are more likely to believe teachers' protestations about their importance in their children's education if these are accompanied by practical suggestions. Hewison and Tizard (1980) provided a fascinating example.

Parents were asked to listen to their infant-age children reading from books they brought home from school. A subsequent study showed that parental listening produced greater gains than provision of extra reading lessons at school from an experienced teacher (Tizard *et al*, 1982). Parents were *not* given elaborate guidance on *how* to listen to their children. More important, the research took place in schools with a multi-ethnic intake in Haringey, a socially disadvantaged part of London. This was precisely the sort of area in which parents would be least likely, according to conventional wisdom, to be able and willing to help in their children's education.

The Haringey research has been confirmed elsewhere (e.g. Widlake and Macleod, 1984) and Young and Tyre (1983) also found benefits for children with specific reading difficulties in their parents listening to their reading. This is a group which is generally thought to need very specialised help. An interesting feature of the Haringey research was that the children's reading improved even if the parents did not understand English. It is not clear how parental involvement in the curriculum may improve children's progress, but elsewhere I have suggested four possibilities (Galloway, 1987):

1. It is well known that skills learned in one context do not necessarily transfer to another. By listening to their children reading from books they bring home from school, parents help to overcome problems of learning transfer.

2. By listening to their children reading parents demonstrate the importance they attach to their progress at school and thus increase their motivation to succeed at school.
3. Arising from the last point, parents who are themselves illiterate often value literacy extremely highly: Friendly encouragement to co-operate with the school is encouraged and leads parents and children to view school attendance in a different light.
4. Establishing co-operative contact with parents and observing the beneficial results on children's progress is likely to change teachers' perceptions of their pupils' parents . . . Children are sensitive to their teacher's attitudes. A sense that their parents and teachers are working together seems likely to contribute to a climate of security favourable to successful learning. (pp. 180–181).

So far we have been talking about parents' involvement at home in the teaching of their children to read. It is not difficult to think of similar opportunities in other areas of the curriculum or in other age-groups. More difficult is provision of opportunities for parents to help in the classroom. This happens in many infant classes, fewer junior classes and scarcely at all in secondary schools. The reasons are not hard to see. The curriculum for older children tends to be more teacher-led, the children themselves may be less dependent on adult help, and they may resent or be embarrassed by the presence of their parents. Providing opportunities for parents to contribute to mainstream school activities can nevertheless be fruitful. Open days when parents are welcome to sit in on any class is a more artificial but still potentially useful exercise.

Parents as students

This will apply in secondary schools rather than primaries, and will be dependent on pupil numbers. Opening GCSE and A level classes to parents wishing to obtain these qualifications is a visible way of demonstrating the school's open-door policy in its service to the community. There may be additional advantages. Working in the school with the pupils, parents (or other adults) see that behaviour is seldom a problem, and can thus scotch the rumours of indiscipline that occasionally circulate in most communities.

Parents' evenings

Teachers' conditions of service now require them to be available to discuss pupils' work with parents. Annual or termly parents' evenings remain one of the most frequent ways of meeting this requirement. They are seldom very satisfactory either for teachers or for parents, but in the absence of more effective and less formal arrangements for parents and teachers to meet, they will doubtless continue. The question, then, is how to make them as satisfactory as possible. Herding everyone into a central hall, for example, may be economical in time when the school's buildings are widely scattered but is inexcusable if there is any better solution. Primary teachers usually expect to have a sample of each child's work available for parents to see in their own classrooms. My strong impression is that secondary teachers more often rely on memory, supplemented by their mark book. It really does not help parents very much to be told their son's marks or place in the form when they have little concept of what these refer to, and are given little if any guidance on how the teacher thinks they may be able to help him in the future.

A further reason for teachers meeting parents in their own classrooms whenever possible it that is gives both teacher and pupils an incentive to review the general appearance of the room. Again, secondary teachers have much to learn from their primary colleagues about effective presentation and display of pupils' work. The value of this is reflected in the evidence that attractive display of children's work is associated with effective schooling in terms of pupils' progress and behaviour (Rutter *et al*, 1979).

Home visits

In most cases a climate of trust and confidence can be achieved when parents visit the school. There are, however, occasions when parents cannot visit the school, either because they are working or because they are suffering from poor health. There are also occasions when teachers may feel that a child's welfare requires a closer understanding of the child's problems than is possible in the more formal setting of the school. In such circumstances a home visit can be useful. Home visiting is not something that all teachers find easy. Visiting with a more experienced colleague can be helpful on the first two or three occasions.

Marland (1985) lists four advantages from discussing a child's welfare in her or his own home. They are:

(i) The school's representative has demonstrated sufficient concern to visit, and this fact alone is encouraging to parents or guardians;

(ii) the pupil's parents or guardians are on *their* home ground, offering *their* hospitality, and this often gives them an added confidence and willingness to share;

(iii) in the home, the centrality of the pupil is symbolically more obvious and powerful than in school, where convenience for the school's system can loom larger;

(iv) only in the pupil's own home setting is it possible to really learn about her or his background sympathetically, and to learn from parents or guardians. (p. 106)

Conclusions

The depth of the suspicion in which parents are held in many schools is reflected in the frequency with which they are seen in staff-rooms. The head of a large multi-ethnic school in Wellington, New Zealand, once remarked that he would know he was running a good school when parents drank as much coffee in the staff-room as teachers. He was not suggesting this as the only measure of the school's effectiveness, but he was making a valid point about the importance of parents and teachers working together and learning from each other.

Recent legislation is requiring schools to be much more sensitive to parents' wishes and priorities than was formerly considered necessary or professionally desirable. The impact of this is only gradually being felt, but the trend will certainly continue for the foreseeable future. Yet at the same time that the government gives parents new opportunities for active involvement in their children's educational welfare, it is expecting teachers to accept new responsibility for their personal and social welfare.

Questions and exercises

1. Debate the motion that: 'Recent legislation has given parents power without responsibility in their children's education'.
2. Role-play a governors' meeting in which parent representatives try to obtain more information about the curriculum from the head and 2 teacher representatives, all of whom see this as their professional preserve.
3. What arrangements does your school make for parents who wish to talk about their children's progress? How do you think parents regard these?
4. Write a letter asking a parent to visit the school to talk about their daughter's bad language.

Recommended reading

Bastiani, J. (Ed.) (1987) *Perspectives on Home-School Relations*. Windsor, NFER-Nelson.
Bastiani, J. (1988) *From Policy to Practice*. Windsor, NFER-Nelson.
Johnson, D. and Ranson, E. (1983) *Family and School*. London, Croom Helm.
Marland, M. (1985) Parents, Schooling and the Welfare of Pupils. In Ribbins, P. (Ed.) *Schooling and Welfare*. Lewes, Falmer.
Topping, K. J. (1986) *Parents as Educators: Training Parents to Teach their Children*. London, Croom Helm.

CHAPTER 8

Using the support services effectively

Introduction

A requirement in any job is for people to recognise their own level of competence. Teachers have responsibilities for aspects of children's welfare which at first sight may appear only indirectly related to their classroom work. Inevitably, they come across problems which they lack either the time or the expertise to tackle. Teachers themselves are generally the first to recognise this, and one might therefore suppose that there would be close co-operation between schools and the educational and social work support services in a climate of mutual understanding and respect. Unfortunately this is not always the case.

Two quite separate scenarios appear from a detailed look at the relationships between schools and the support services. Together they may appear to put both sides in a kind of "Catch 22": a situation in which whatever they do can be criticised. The first problem relates to the open or covert friction that sometimes exists. Stereotypes abound. Teachers feel that educational psychologists and social workers move with almost perverse slowness in situations when the child's welfare requires quick decisions. In their charitable moments they attribute delays to a heavy case-load, but then claim to observe little or no sense of urgency even when the wheels have ground into motion. Teachers also criticise social workers for placing the wishes of parents and the perceived needs of the family ahead of the welfare of the child.

Social workers have their stereotypes too. Teachers are seen as excessively preoccupied with problems of discipline and control, overlooking the personal and social welfare of the individual in their concern for an orderly classroom climate. They are also seen as insensitive to strengths within the child's family, preferring to dwell on problems which may well be transitory. Related to this, teachers are seen as intolerant of cultures which differ from their own, expecting children to conform to their own middle-class expectations and values. Finally, teachers are seen as ignorant about the potentially adverse effects of removing children from home.

These *are* stereotypes, but they are stereotypes which strike disquieteningly familiar notes in many experienced teachers and in members of the support services. They constitute one of the scenarios referred to earlier. The second is more complex and is evident when teachers and members of the support services *are* working closely together. In *this* case, a close look sometimes suggests that the co-operation exists more for the benefits of the professionals concerned than of their clients. It is in this sense that the relationship between teachers and the support services can find itself in a Catch 22: not to co-operate is pernicious; to co-operate and work closely together is equally pernicious!

In this chapter we will explore this problem, and argue that it can be avoided. We shall start by reviewing the formal role of the existing LEA support services and considering how these are likely to be affected by the 1988 Education Reform Act. We shall next look briefly at services outside the LEA with which teachers most often come into contact. The final part of the chapter will examine some of the pit-falls in interdisciplinary co-operation and propose a model for a relationship which may benefit professionals and children.

LEA support services

Perhaps the first thing to acknowledge about the support services is that the notion of support is tinged with that of care which in turn is linked with that of control. The idea of LEA-funded support-services striving disinterestedly to support similarly disinterested teachers in carrying out their work really does not bear close scrutiny. To start with, members of the support services do not only visit schools at the invitation of teachers. They also visit as part of their responsibilities to the LEA.

This is most evident in the case of advisors/inspectors, but also applies to educational psychologists and educational welfare officers. If the LEA receives a complaint from parents that their child's educational needs are being met inadequately, this complaint will be investigated by members of the support services. The same applies if members of the public persistently complain about indiscipline by the school's pupils in the playground or during the lunch hour. At a different level, the LEA is responsible for the general conduct of its schools and for the work carried out in them. In the same way that HMI are still conventionally thought of as the 'eyes and ears' of the DES, the support services are the eyes and ears of the LEA. They also have responsibilities for initiating change. Even with the introduction of the national curriculum, LEAs retain a potentially important role in curriculum development. To say that curriculum development is 'supported' by advisers and, in some

LEAs, educational psychologists, overlooks the pressures the LEA can exert on teachers to follow its guidelines. Logically, an effective LEA policy cannot exist without restricting the autonomy of schools and teachers.

The support services, then, have a normative function, to maintain and develop teachers' work according to guidelines, or norms, proposed by central government and by the LEA. It is important not to be too deterministic about this. It is not their only function. They also exist to encourage and support 'grass-roots' initiatives. Yet even here their normative role is evident since they must inevitably be selective in the initiatives they encourage. A general adviser in the commuter-belt counties of South-East England would be unlikely to encourage peace studies in secondary schools.

The normative role is seen most starkly in the case of education welfare officers and educational psychologists. It is all very well in theory to say that their work is concerned with the social, personal, educational or psychological welfare of children. In practice, what constitutes welfare is influenced, if not determined, by the dominant culture. Members of the LEA support services are LEA officers, answerable to their employers as well as to their clients. This argument will become clearer when we look at the role of the three support services with which teachers most frequently have contacts.

Advisers/inspectors

In the 1950's and 1960s most LEAs employed 'inspectors' whose job, broadly, was to carry out at local level the responsibilities that HMI carried out at national level. In the 1970s these inspectors were renamed as advisers in a majority of LEAs and expected to play an active part in INSET and curriculum development. Today some LEAs are going full cycle, and once more appointing inspectors. The change in name reflects a change in emphasis and public image as much as in actual function. Throughout the late 1960s and 1970s education was a growth industry. Apart from a handful of sociologists, few people questioned the doctrine of teacher autonomy. The emphasis was on helping teachers to achieve the high standards to which they and society professed to aspire. Throughout the 1980s the mood changed. Increasingly, the emphasis was on accountability: of teachers to parents and school governors, of schools to their local community, of LEAs to central government. It is not surprising, then, that the emphasis should swing back to the inspectorial function.

How this will be carried out in the wake of the 1988 Education

Reform Act remains unclear. In the past advisers/LEA inspectors have had considerable influence on appointment of staff, many of them spending substantial time on appointment panels. The introduction of local financial management of schools may well reduce this influence, since governors will have almost complete control over the appointment of staff. On the other hand, it is not impossible that local financial management may actually increase the adviser's influence, since 'lay' governors may feel the need for professional advice.

It is, however, clear that advisers will play increasing roles in monitoring standards in schools, especially with regard to targets of attainment and national testing. They will also play a leading part in the LEA's INSET programme leading to the introduction of the national curriculum. They may see themselves as having general oversight of the school's social and moral climate, but their involvement in problems concerning the welfare of individual pupils will generally be limited.

Educational welfare officers (EWOs)

The educational welfare service has been, and remains, the Cinderella of the LEA support services. Historically, it has been concerned principally with school attendance and is always involved in decisions to take legal action over unjustified absences from school. The Franks Report (Local Government Training Board, 1972) recommended that social work training should be recognised as the basic qualification for entry to the service. Earlier the Seebohm Report (DHSS 1968) had recommended that the service should combine with the proposed new local authority departments of social services. This never happened, nor has the Certificate of Qualification in Social Work come to be widely accepted as the basic qualification for entry. There are three reasons. First, many EWOs were anxious about losing their professional identity in large social services departments. Second, schools were worried about the prospect of losing 'their' EWOs. This comes back to the question of control. Head teachers tended to see the EWO as a person whose principal responsibility was to the school. If they were taken over by social services, their loyalties and priorities might change. Third, local councils were anxious about the financial implications of a move towards a fully qualified service.

Several authors have drawn attention to the potential role of EWOs in identifying child welfare problems at an early stage (e.g. MacMillan, 1980; Fitzherbert, 1977). Teachers are in a uniquely favourable position to observe the effects of neglect or ill-treatment, and the education welfare service is in a similarly favourable position to follow up these suspicions. How far EWOs are able to act as the frontline of the welfare network must, however, depend largely on how broadly their job is defined. If they are seen simply as 'school bobbies', they are unlikely to have much credibility with parents, teachers or social workers. In this case, their role will continue to be defined in terms of investigating and dealing with attendance problems. In principle, however, they could play a more constructive and more important part in the work of schools. This would require them to respond to a wider range of problems than school attendance. More important, it would involve them in bringing to teachers' attention problems in their pupils' lives outside schools which might be affecting their progress or adjustment at school. In other words, EWOs would be seen as having a part to play in the child's teaching and management at school. This is a far cry from the school bobby image in which their role ceases when the child is back at school.

Unfortunately the DES appears distinctly unenthusiastic about developments in the educational welfare service. HMI (1984) reported on their inspection of the service in eight LEAs. They noted that teachers often held stereotyped and incorrect views of the EWOs, for example that many had served as police officers. They also noted poor relationships between the educational welfare service and local authority social services departments. Rather lamely, the report concluded that more discussion was needed on the social work of EWOs, HMI were, however, clear that control of the service should remain with LEAs. The DES (1985b) responded to the inspectors' report by issuing a draft circular which stated:

(a) that the main objective of the service was "the promotion of the important educational objective of regular school attendance" (p. l);
(b) that "the primary responsibility for links with all parents rests with teachers", not with EWOs (p. l);
(c) that the service existed to serve the child in relation to school attendance, not the whole family;
(d) that there should be a balance between officers with social work training and officers selected for their maturity and experience.

Responses to the DES draft circular from EWOs and social workers were uniformly hostile, though some teacher associations saw virtues in continuing to be able to pass attendance problems over to the EWO. The service remains under-funded with limited opportunities for in-service training in most LEAs. How it will be affected by local management of schools as proposed by the 1986 Education Reform Act is not yet clear. It seems probable, though that it will remain as a service provided centrally by the LEA, at least in the short term.

Educational psychologists

Educational psychologists face many of the same problems of role confusion as EWOs. They might not welcome the comparison, though. While EWOs are professionally the least qualified group within the education service, educational psychologists are probably the most highly qualified. They are normally required to hold a good honours degree in psychology, a professional teaching qualification, a minimum of two years' teaching experience and postgraduate training, usually at Masters level, in educational psychology. There are now well over 1,000 educational psychologists in England and Wales. The Warnock Report (DES, 1978) recommended that they should be employed at a ratio of 1:6,000 children aged 0–19, though 1:8,000 of compulsory school age is probably nearer the national average.

The only statutory responsibility of educational psychologists comes in the 1981 Education Act which requires them to contribute to the formal assessment of children's special educational needs. In some LEAs this appears to represent the major part of their work. In others they are much more readily available to schools for informal discussions on a range of questions. These usually have at least an indirect relationship to learning or adjustment problems, though not necessarily a direct one. They have, for example, been involved in evaluating alternatives to the traditional parents' evening and in developing equal opportunities policies. More frequently, they visit school to discuss individual children at an informal level.

Two principal tensions are evident in the work of educational psychologists. First, since the 1970s many of them have been exploring ways to work with teachers on projects that have a wider educational significance than their work with individual pupils (e.g. Gillam, 1978; Cox and Lavelle, 1982). Yet in many LEAs the effect of the 1981 Education Act has been to force them back into a working mode in which most of their time is spent on the assessment of individual children. Second, there is continual and inevitable tension between their responsibilities to their employing authority to the schools they visit and to the children they see. As Goacher *et al* (1988) points out, they are open to pressure to define a child's special needs in the light of available provision. The unspoken, but sometimes very explicit message is: don't identify needs which we might have difficulty in meeting without incurring extra expenditure.

A word is needed on the limitations inherent in the assessment of individual children. The school's and the LEA's expectation is that the *child* has problems. Yet in practice it is impossible to assess a child's learning or behavioural difficulties without also considering the context in which these are evident. Hence, assessment of individual children can reveal limitations in the organisation, curriculum, resources and teaching methods in their schools. Drawing attention to these without irrevocably antagonising the school's teachers requires diplomatic skills of a high order. Failure to draw attention to them implies acquiescence in a cosy professional consensus which sees the problem as located in the child and/or the family rather than in the school or the classroom. This tension is also evident in the contacts between schools and support services independent of the LEA.

Other support services

Many of the tensions that may arise between teachers and members of the LEA support services are also apparent in contacts with services independent of the LEA. A succession of reports has criticised the lack of co-operation between schools and social work agencies, for example the DHSS (1974) Report on Maria Colwell, the London Borough of Brent (1985) Report on Jasmine Beckford and the London Borough of Greenwich (1987) Report on Kimberley Carlisle.

Teachers have a responsibility for initiating contacts with services outside the LEA if they suspect that the child is at risk of physical, emotional or sexual abuse. Yet social workers also have a responsibility for initiating contacts with schools when they suspect that children's educational progress is being affected by their home circumstances. At the very least they must explore the possibility of the school making additional support or resources available. This could range from allowing the child to do homework in the library in the lunch hour, to careful monitoring of attendance on days when PE is time-tabled and a parent might keep their children at home to prevent detection of bruising when they changed.

In addition to meetings with local authority social workers, teachers may have contacts with voluntary agencies such as the NSPCC, Barnardo's and Family Service Unit. The Police, too, may be called on by teachers to investigate offences committed outside the school. This is a sensitive area, on which teachers should follow the LEA's guidelines. From a purely legal point of view, teachers are *in loco parentis* and may therefore ask or permit the police to interview a pupil. In practice, hearing that their child has been interviewed without their knowledge or consent is almost guaranteed to arouse parents' antagonism and mistrust of teachers.

The people with whom teachers have most frequent contacts are doctors and nurses in the school health service. Although employed by the Area Health Authority, they are based in schools. In the past nurses have often been dismissed as 'nit nurses', but schools should be able to negotiate a more extensive and constructive role for them. Many school nurses contribute to the school's health education programme, and often are seen as a valuable source of counselling support for pupils. The role of school doctors, too, is changing, with less emphasis on routine screening for visual and auditory impairment, and more on monitoring the health of pupils with medical problems and advising teachers on the educational implications.

The school health service may also have access to child psychiatrists, qualified doctors specialising in the treatment of emotional and behavioural problems. Referral to a child psychiatrist requires the family doctor's consent, and usually can only be made by the school doctor or educational psychologists. In some LEA's they work as part of a child guidance clinic team, staffed jointly by the Area Health Authority and the LEA. In other areas they work through the child psychiatry outpatient clinics of local hospitals. As in child guidance clinics, most families referred to out-patient clinics are seen by a multi-disciplinary team consisting of child psychiatrist, educational psychologist and social workers.

Specialist psychiatric treatment may be necessary when the child's behavioural or learning difficulty may have a medical origin. School doctors and educational psychologists should be able to advise on this. Although some clinic teams are trying to become responsive to the needs of schools, most of their activities remain clinic-based. The usefulness of clinic-based treatment for children with social or behavioural problems has been strongly questioned (e.g. Tizard, 1973). Families with social problems associated with poor housing or unemployment may have great difficulty in keeping appointments at clinics which are often based in leafy suburbs. Moreover, the chances of behaviour problems *in* the classroom clearing up as a result of clinical treatment outside it are not high (e.g. Levitt, 1963).

This raises questions both about the frequency and about the quality of contacts between teachers and members of the support services. Mutual respect and understanding is not ensured by regular and informal contact, but cannot realistically be expected to develop without it. We turn shortly to the obstacles to inter-disciplinary co-operation, but first need to consider the implications of the Education Reform Act.

The Education Reform Act

We have already hinted at likely implications of the Act, and are concerned in this section mainly with its probable impact on pupils experiencing educational or social problems. We shall look at these in the light of the relationships between schools and the support services.

Many critics have argued that the national curriculum will create increased problems for children with special needs. Brennan (1987) and Peter (1988) for example, claim that it will result in a narrower curriculum for these pupils, with reduced choice. It is difficult to see the logic behind their argument, since the Act is explicit in requiring that *all* pupils have access to the national curriculum except for those who have been explicitly exempted from it. Moreover, a consistent criticism of the curriculum for pupils with special needs has been its narrowness compared with that provided for pupils in the mainstream (e.g. Galloway and Goodwin, 1987). The 'alternative' curricula provided for pupils of below average ability in the mainstream have also aroused strong opposition (e.g. Hargreaves, 1982). The Act should result in a broadening, not narrowing, of the curriculum for the large majority of pupils with special needs in ordinary schools.

The Act does, however, make provision for exemptions from the national curriculum. The statement of special educational needs, produced following formal assessment under the 1981 Education Act, can exempt a child from part or all of its require-ments. In addition, exemptions may be permitted 'in cases or circumstances' yet to be specified in regulations. Exemptions in this group will not, however, be permitted to last for more than six months and are intended to enable a formal assessment to be carried out. Nevertheless, they may be quite numerous. The publication of their school's results in the national testing programme, at 7, 11, 14 and 16 seems likely to encourage head-teachers to seek exemptions from the national curriculum, and hence from national testing, for pupils whose scores would drag down the school's results. The same fear may lead head teachers of grant-maintained schools to refuse entry to pupils with special needs, though this problem may have been exaggerated as governors must specify their school's admission policies when applying for grant-maintained status.

What remains absolutely clear, though, is that the national curriculum and associated national testing will increase rather than reduce calls on the educational support services. LEAs will increasingly be calling on advisers to monitor standards and assist in teacher appraisal schemes. Schools will be calling on them for assistance in implementing the national curriculum. Educational psychologists will increasingly find themselves carrying out formal assessments of pupils for whom exemption from the national curriculum has been requested. Educational welfare officers, too, may find themselves under increased pressure to respond to teachers' anxiety about the impact of pupils' prolonged absence on their future test results.

The support services, then, should anticipate increased demands as a result of the Act. This does not mean that they will simply be providing more of the same. How their relationships with schools develop will depend largely on how the government implements the provision for local management of schools. In a report commissioned by the DES, the management consultants Coopers and Lybrand (1988) recommended that funding of advisory/inspector services should remain the LEA's responsibility, at least in the short term. They suggest that funding of school psychological, educational welfare and medical services should remain the LEA's responsibility indefinitely on the grounds that schools might:

. . . . under-purchase such services and seek to make do with staff less professionally qualified, perhaps at the expense of the pupils concerned. Further, unless schools were sure that the formula allocation of resources adequately provided for such resources, there might be an unfortunate tendency for schools to be more reluctant to accept pupils who might need such services – in so far as schools were in a position to influence entry (para. 2.65, p. 17).

It remains unclear how the government will implement local management of schools, though by the time this book is published LEAs should have produced proposals for consideration by the DES. It seems probable, though, that an increasingly contractual relationship will develop between schools and the various services provided centrally by the LEA. This carries the potential for abrasive friction as well as for constructive co-operation.

Interdisciplinary co-operation – devoutly to be wished?

Interdisciplinary co-operation is in danger of becoming an unquestionable article of faith. The Warnock Report (DES, 1978) devoted a chapter to it. The 1981 Education Act advocated it. Successive commisions of enquiry have attributed tragedies resulting in children's death or, in some of the Cleveland child sexual abuse cases, their inappropriate removal from home, to the lack of it. The DES (1988) and the DHSS (1988) have issued circulars calling for it. Yet *it* – interdisciplinary cooperation – appears almost as hard to achieve as the abolition of poverty. Why, then, is it so hard to achieve? And if *it* is achieved, can we be sure we have won a famous victory?

Obstacles to interdisciplinary co-operation

Superficially, it is easy to see how failures of co-operation between teachers and the educational, medical and social work support services occur. From a class teacher's point of view, it takes anything from 6 months to 2 years for a child's special educational needs to be assessed and a statement prepared. Thus, the teacher who refers a child may feel she is unlikely to derive much benefit. Head teachers often feel that social workers, like the Police, are never there when you need them. Yet if the problem went no deeper than this, it would be relatively simple to solve. The real problems lie in the conflicting interests of different professional groupings.

The notion that everyone in the teaching, child health and caring profession is working disinterestedly in the children's best interests is comforting but does not stand close scrutiny. Tomlinson (1982) has demonstrated that the history of special education is littered with the debris of infighting as different professional groups struggle for supremacy. The same is true of other areas of social policy. Professions differ in status. Among the LEA support services this ranges from the humble, or downtrodden, educational welfare service to the advisers/inspectors who write references for teachers' applications for promotion and sign their letters Director of Education. Not only do professions differ in status, but the relative pecking order also changes. Throughout the 1970s the influence of educational psychologists in the assessment of children's special needs grew, largely at the expense of school doctors. Within the teaching profession, science and technology now hold the dominant positions once possessed by the classics.

Tension then, if not outright rivalry, are inherent in the very existence of different professional groupings working in the same field. Each develops its own professional knowledge, with associated 'professional' qualifications which effectively exclude outsiders. The British Psychological Society recently persuaded the Privy Council to amend its charter so that only approved members could legally describe themselves as 'chartered psychologists'. The motive, ostensively, was to protect the public from unqualified practitioners. Yet some of the treatments offered by highly qualified psychologists are notorious for the lack of evidence for their effectiveness, psychotherapy being the most obvious example. Moreover, there is no prospect of any consensus within the society as to which form of treatment would be indicated for any particular psychological problem. Perhaps it is unfair to use psychologists as an example, though, since similar points could be made about many other professions.

Developing a specific knowledge base and professional expertise leads inevitably to social as well as professional exclusiveness.

It is unhelpful to think of this process as a conspiracy. A person's sense of personal identity depends largely on his or her memberships of social groups. The family provides one social group, and the office another. Further, people's self-esteem depends largely on feeling they are doing a useful job with an adequate level of security. This applies as much to social workers and teachers as to joiners and boiler makers. Yet each profession's exclusiveness relates to professed expertise in dealing with the same children and families as other professional groups, who have developed their own exclusiveness.

We cannot, then, be surprised, if they see the same situation in different ways. This becomes even more probable given the different priorities of teachers and the support services. For a social worker or an educational psychologist, the first priority is likely to be the welfare of the individual child and her or his family. Whatever they may say publicly, this is not and cannot be a teacher's first priority, which is to the overall welfare of the class as a whole. This is much more than an academic quibble. Children facing special social or educational difficulties are demanding of the teacher's time, and may present behavioural problems which disrupt the class. Yet if teachers define a problem solely in terms of a child's welfare, when their real, and perhaps legitimate, concern is for the other children, or perhaps even for their own stress level, barriers to effective communication become almost insurmountable.

Pitfalls in interdisciplinary co-operation

Assuming all these problems are overcome it does not follow that teachers and members of the support services will necessarily co-operate in the best interest of the child and family. Pratt (1983) has described a meeting in which confidential information about older boys in the family was passed between professionals in the parents' absence. The plea of the professional concerned, that she did not want the boy who was being discussed to be judged by his brothers' standards, rang distinctly hollow. All too often, irrelevant information about a family is circulated either with no clear thought as to its purpose or, worse, in the hope that it will lead to the decision favoured by a particular professional person.

A related scenario is when an interdisciplinary case conference:

deteriorates into a hand-wringing session in which everyone commiserates on the insolubility of the problem. This frequently follows an unproductive exchange of information. It engenders a comforting, if illogical, feeling that since everyone agrees, the problem really must be insoluble, and therefore no-one's personal responsibility.

(Galloway, 1985, p. 124)

Thus may professionals present a united front against their

clients. Yet EWOs and educational psychologists may find themselves in an impossible position. The problems in arranging a child's return to school after a period of truancy illustrate the dilemma.

> In theory, EWOs have a good deal of autonomy. In practice, criticisms from head teachers will make their life extremely difficult. Moreover, they know that their chances of gaining cooperation from teachers . . . is entirely dependent on their acceptance as members of an extended staff team. Hence, any actions or suggestions which might threaten acceptance have to be regarded with great caution. Accepting the school's perception of poor attendance – for example that it is illegal and/or that it results from individual or family deviance or psychopathology becomes a necessity, at least initially. The reasons are twofold:
> (i) acceptance depends on "not rocking the boat" too much;
> (ii) without acceptance they are in no position to negotiate changes in the school to facilitate a child's return. The contradiction in the argument is that the procedures adopted to gain acceptance largely negate the EWO's role as a change agent or child advocate within the school.
>
> (Galloway, 1985, P. 125)

Interdisciplinary co-operation, then, is more complex and potentially more contentious than judges and politicians would have us believe. Committees of the great and the good are seldom well placed to appreciate either the obstacles to their proposals or the pitfalls in them. We should not, however, regard this gloomy picture as unchangeable.

Towards a 3-way partnership

Who is the expert?

Expertise, unfortunately, is not acquired just by being considered an expert. Being considered an expert depends as much on other people's perceptions of the job you are doing as on your own ability in the job. Expert status, then, is bestowed, and refers to the person's primary responsibilities for a job. Expertise in that job is acquired by training and by experience. I wish to argue that inter-disciplinary cooperation depends on the class or subject teacher being seen as the expert in the classroom.

Mutual trust depends on mutual respect. In the context of relationships between teachers and other professionals this implies that teachers' primary responsibility for their pupils' behaviour and progress is respected. It is not always easy to recognise how quickly this can be undermined. Terms like 'under the psychologist', 'dyslexic', 'a problem family', 'special educational needs' have the effect of devolving responsibility from the teacher on to another expert: 'this is a special case; I haven't got the training or expertise to deal with it; someone else must be better qualified'. If, though, the teacher is to be seen as the expert in the classroom, what role is there for highly trained members of the support services?

The meaning of partnership

Partnership implies equality. There are times when the support services use their knowledge and resources to provide something outside the classroom that the teacher cannot offer. Protecting a child through removal from home, or the offer of family psychotherapy, are examples. On other occasions, the support services' task is to help the teachers – the classroom experts – in their work with a child. Clearly, social work agencies independent of the LEA are more likely to be offering assistance outside the classroom, while many educational psychologists see their principal task in terms of enabling teachers to work more effectively in the classroom.

In practice this distinction can become blurred. Even if social workers are undertaking family casework in the home, seeing the child at school may give them additional relevant information. Similarly, from their home-based casework, social workers may be able, with parents' and children's permission, to help teachers recognise the problems children are experiencing at school.

The point here is that besides implying equality, partnership implies accountability. Thus, effective interdisciplinary co-operation requires the various parties to feel accountable to their colleagues as well as to their clients. An example from the work of an educational psychologist illustrates this.

Karen, aged 11, had made little progress over the previous three terms and often appeared uninterested, even resentful, having previously been a lively, enthusiastic pupil. The school's educational psychologist already knew the family, and in discussion with her teacher suggested she might benefit from being seated at a different table, and from being given responsibilities for updating the display in a corner of the classroom. Karen welcomed the move and the additional attention from her teacher, but there were still frequent occasions when she seemed sullen and resentful, at best apathetic to the work the class was doing. Her teacher's message to the psychologist was simple: 'I've done what we agreed, but it hasn't really changed the situation. What else can you suggest?' In other words, the teacher and the psychologist saw themselves as accountable to each other.

In this particular case, more detailed observation in the classroom revealed a vocal minority of pupils who felt they had outgrown the primary school, and a less vocal minority who were becoming increasingly anxious at the horror stories they were hearing from their older 'friends' about life in the secondary school. Karen was in the second group. The psychologist tackled the short-term problem facing Karen by arranging for her to visit the secondary school with her parents and to spend a day at the secondary school in the company of a friend in her first year there (see Delamont and Gatton, 1986). The long-term problems involved the fourth year curriculum in the junior school, which the pupils saw as 'just the same as last year, miss', and the school's procedures for primary-secondary transfer. These, clearly, required careful discussion to which both the psychologist and the school's adviser were able to contribute.

Karen's case raises a further issue in co-operation between teachers and other professionals, namely the role of parents and of children. Ideally the sense of accountability between a teacher and another professional extends to the way they both work with parents and with children. Professional relationships can easily exclude the people they are designed to help. Occasionally, as in decisions on child abuse cases, this is difficult to avoid. Nevertheless we should not underestimate the willingness both of parents and of children to be involved in the decisions that affect them. Insensitivity to this basic principle led to the tragedy of inappropriate and heavy-handed intervention in some of the Cleveland child sexual abuse cases. The tragedy lay not only in the suffering of families in which no abuse had occurred, but also in the set-back resulting from the subsequent furore to the growing recognition of the scale of child sexual abuse.

Conclusions

We do neither ourselves nor our pupils a service by underestimating the obstacles to effective partnership with members of other professional groups. Working with colleagues in different professions is at least as challenging for both sides as working with parents. Working together exposes not only the professional expertise of each party, but also their limitations. It requires a level of openness with other professionals and with parents that can make us feel both visible and vulnerable. For this reason, effective co-operation is unlikely unless there is a climate of mutual trust and respect within the school's staff. This needs a chapter of its own.

Questions and exercises

1. As a class/subject teacher, write a 'job description' specifying the service you would like from your school's:

(a) EWO

(b) educational psychologist.

2. Debate the motion that: 'Under Local Financial Management schools should be free to buy in the services of advisers, EWOs and educational psychologists as and when they see fit.'

3. What advice have you received, or should you have received about children in your class with visual or hearing impairment? Is there a need to redefine the role of the school doctor or nurse?

4. How far can/should teachers' own values influence the decision to refer a case of possible emotional neglect to the local social services department?

5. Role play the initial meeting between a teacher whose life is being made a misery by a child's difficult behaviour and an educational psychologist who, while sympathetic, suspects that part of the problem may lie in poor classroom management.

6. Is there a valid distinction, as suggested in the text, between being an expert and having expertise?

7. In what sense may teachers and social workers employed by the local authority feel themselves accountable to each other?

8. Think of children you are currently teaching, or whom you have taught in the last two years, who have been referred to members of the LEA support services and/or to social work services. Now consider the following questions:

(a) What have been the benefits for the children themselves?

(b) What have been the benefits for you as their teacher?

(c) In what sense, if any, was there a partnership between you and the agency concerned?

Recommended reading

Fitzherbert, K. (1977) *Child Care Services and the Teacher*. London, Maurice Temple Smith.

Galloway, D. (1985) *Schools and Persistent Absentees*. Oxford, Pergamon (Chapter 8).

Goacher, B., Evans, J., Welton, J. and Wedell, K. (1988) *Policy and Provision for Special Educational Needs: Implementing the 1981 Education Act*. London, Cassell.

Her Majesty's Inspectors of Schools (1984) *The Educational Welfare Services: An Enquiry into Eight LEAs*. London, DES.

CHAPTER 9

Working with colleagues

Introduction

The relationships between members of a school's staff is a neglected issue in the literature on pupil welfare. Teachers cannot realistically hope to foster their pupils' personal and social development, let alone to maintain effective working relationships with members of other professional groups if their own relationships are fraught with tension. Welfare aspects in any teacher's job are potentially stressful. They are also potentially a source of stimulation and job satisfaction. Working relationships with colleagues can compound the stress inherent in classroom teaching or can help to create a climate which is both stimulating and supportive.

In this chapter we look at how relationships with colleagues are likely, for better or worse, to affect children's welfare. We return once again to recent government initiatives and the impact these are likely to have on relationships within a school's staff. Finally, we consider the sort of guidance that class or subject teachers might reasonably expect from senior colleagues.

Tensions in relationships with colleagues

Nias (1980) interviewed newly-appointed graduate primary school teachers about their head teacher's leadership styles. These teachers expressed strong dissatisfaction when heads were passive, emphasised the 'social distance' between themselves and their staff, were administratively inefficient or authoritarian in their professional relationships. In contrast, Nias identified as 'positive' leadership styles characterised by high professional standards, consultation with colleagues and active support for their professional development.

Interestingly, these teachers did not report positive leadership from the head as a major source of job satisfaction. Rather, the head's leadership style created a climate in which its satisfaction was possible. This is consistent with the results of other studies which show that teachers' job satisfaction is closely linked to the basic, or intrinsic aspects of their work, namely children's progress and relationship with children (e.g. Holdaway, 1978;

Sergiovanni, 1976; Galloway *et al*, 1985). Dissatisfaction on the other hand, arises from conditions at work rather than from the work itself. These could include the low public esteem in which teachers are held, inadequate salaries and poor resources for use in the classroom, as well as the head's leadership.

Tensions in relations with senior colleagues can be a source of anxiety, for beginning teachers, not just of dissatisfaction (Coates and Thoresen, 1976). A contemptuously dismissive term heard in many secondary school staffrooms in Britain is 'the hierarchy', used when referring to decisions made by an implicitly impersonal senior management team.

It is not only newly-appointed teachers who suffer. It seems likely that poor relationships with colleagues are linked to the experience of 'burn-out' in older teachers. Edelwich and Brodsky (1980) described four stages of disillusionment in the helping professions, including teaching. After an initial stage of enthusiasm, a period of stagnation sets in, followed by frustration. In the final stage, of apathy, teachers become indifferent to the quality of their own performance. While there is little experimental evidence at least in Britain, the concept of burn-out is useful in showing how stress in teaching may be seen as a progressive phenomenon. We need, therefore, to ask how relationships between teachers interact with the potentially stressful aspects of their work to result, eventually, in the apathy of 'burn-out'. More important, we need to ask how it may be prevented.

The privacy of the classroom

Teaching the core curriculum areas appears to be associated with feelings of stress less frequently than situations involving problems of control and class management. Thus, children's learning and behavioural problems are the most frequent sources of stress in day-to-day teaching (Pratt, 1978), though occasional events such as interviews with parents and class trips were reported as very stressful or extremely stressful by up to 30 per cent of primary teachers in New Zealand (Galloway *et al*, 1985). In contrast teaching reading or Maths was reported as stressful by only 17 per cent. Yet children's behaviour and progress cannot be seen in isolation from the nature of relationships between colleagues.

Primary teachers in Britain have been reported as finding open-plan classes more stressful than the conventional 'single cell' classroom (Bennett, 1980). The reverse was the case in New Zealand where teachers in open-plan classrooms reported significantly less stress from staff relationships, children's behaviour and progress and the visits of inspectors. It seems likely that these results reflect the professional cultures of primary teachers in the two countries. In New Zealand each primary teacher is expected to form part of a 'syndicate', or small team of teachers working with a defined age-range. While there are obviously variations in how effectively this works, the clear expectation is that syndicate members will work together to produce mutually-agreed programmes of work, to discuss professional issues and to review children's progress. In this climate, open-plan classes could be seen as an opportunity to build on an underlying co-operative ethos, and to enhance the support teachers could provide for each other.

In contrast, small groups of teachers who meet regularly to plan programmes of work for their classes are not so frequently found in British primary schools. The professional culture emphasises each teacher's responsibility for his or her class, rather than membership of a co-operative team. Shortly before writing this, I had a letter from a former PGCE student describing how she was left with minimal resources to sink or swim in her first year of teaching. It is worth mentioning only because it happens so frequently. In this underlying climate the close working relationships required in open-plan teaching present a threat, rather than an opportunity to build on existing ways of working.

As always, there are exceptions. Some teachers in New Zealand recalled horror stories of disastrous personal and professional relationships in open-plan classes. Some teachers in Britain talk of open-plan classes as the most exciting and enjoyable they have taught. There is, nevertheless, an important point to be made about the 'professional autonomy' which British teachers have guarded so zealously and, until recent years, so successfully. While possibly overestimating the level of co-operation in some primary schools, Hargreaves (1982) puts his finger on the problem:

Secondary school teachers, much more than their colleagues in primary schools or universities, do not like being observed. For them, teaching is like sexual activity: it is a highly intimate act, best conducted in private, and to be watched by intruders is to inhibit one's performance. The root of this sensitivity is to be found in competence anxieties. Observers are likely to make judgements on one's teaching abilities, and so their presence lays one open to potential criticism. Observation will be evaluative, and implicit and unspoken judgements by witnesses are threatening. Autonomy, then, is the polite word used to mask teacher's evaluative apprehension and to serve as a rationale for excluding observers.

(p. 206)

This is, as Hargreaves admits, a caricature, but caricatures are recognisable, not least to the people they portray. In many schools, teachers hesitate to seek advice from colleagues for fear of being thought incompetent. For their part, other staff hesitate to offer guidance for fear of implying that they think their colleague is incompetent. Nowhere is this pattern more frequently evident than with children with behavioural and learning difficulties. Thus, the 'evaluative apprehension' which maintains the privacy of the classroom deprives teachers of the most obvious and potentially most potent source of support, from their own colleagues, in dealing with the most frequent causes of stress in their day-to-day work. It is just possible, that this may gradually be changing.

Impact of recent government initiatives

In spite of the rhetoric of professional autonomy, teachers' ability to determine their own mode of working has always been limited. At classroom level, pupils can exert a profound influence on how a teacher works as Riseborough (1985) shows in his accounts of 'teacher mincers', pupils with minimal interest in the official aims of the school. Members of a school's middle and senior management have a critical role in creating an open climate, responsive to the needs of staff as well as of pupils. Yet national policy, too, plays a part in staff relationships within a school.

Publication of public examination results, and the proposed national testing programme makes schools more accountable to parents and more vulnerable in their local communities. This could lead to a witch-hunt to root out the alleged incompetents. Alternatively, it could lead head teachers to develop more collegial ways of working, with a growing emphasis on teachers' mutual responsibility to and for each other as well as to their pupils. The new GCSE curricula, together with the national curriculum, illustrate the importance of planning and evaluation involving groups of teachers working together. The old notion of the individual teacher responsible only for his or her subject was never very convincing, and today seems quite untenable. Apart from anything else, teachers will soon be required to take part in a national appraisal scheme, and are already expected to co-operate with colleagues in five days annually of school-based INSET. There remains almost unlimited scope for subverting these initiatives. Many providers of school-based INSET are familiar with the direct and indirect strategies teachers in some schools have adopted to express their resentment at 'compulsory' INSET. Yet this hostility is not inevitable, as is demonstrated in schools in which teachers are successfully creating a more open, supportive and constructively critical climate.

What guidance should class teachers expect from colleagues?

More has been written about what senior staff should expect from their less experienced colleagues than vice-versa. Yet teachers on the main professional grade, irrespective of seniority and experience, may have more scope for influencing senior staff than they realise. There is an interesting parallel here between teachers' and pupils' learning strategies. A frequent characteristic of 'unsuccessful' pupils is the poor use they make of the school's resources, in particular its teachers. Learning to be a pupil is not as straightforward as it may sound. Clearly, it involves learning what curricula and extra-curricula resources the school has to offer. Less obviously, but just as important, is the ability to seek feedback, or guidance, from an appropriate teacher, for example on a specific curriculum problem, a personal matter or a question of option or career choice. Further, 'guidance' may be a euphemism for criticism. Pupils' success in a school may rest heavily on their ability to interpret criticism as guidance on how to find a solution to a particular problem. Anyone with experience in teaching pupils of lower ability will know children who seem to internalise feed-back, seeing it as a statement about themselves rather than as guidance on how to tackle a specific task successfully.

In other words, learning how to seek and use the knowledge, expertise and guidance that their teachers can offer is central in learning to be a pupil. In the same way, learning to use senior colleagues effectively may be central to a teacher's success in the school. We shall consider this at two levels. The first is a practical one, involving contacts with senior colleagues, and the second a theoretical one relating to the teacher's sense of personal and professional responsibility.

Using the hierarchy

An MA student recently claimed that the Roman Catholic Church had five professional grades: Pope, cardinal, archbishop, bishop and priest; yet his school with thirty members of staff had eight; head, deputy, teachers on each of the five incentive allowances and teachers on the main professional grade. He may have over-simplified the hierarchy of the Roman Catholic Church, but he was implicitly making a valid point about the complex hierarchical structure in schools. Few initial teacher training or INSET courses address the question of how to use the hierarchy effectively. This is partly a question of deciding when to go beyond one's immediate head of department or, in a pastoral team, head of year.

Head teachers who by-pass Assistant Education Officers (AEOs) by taking problems straight to the Director of Education rapidly find themselves becoming unpopular with the AEOs who have day-to-day responsibility for the school's administration. They may also find that the director's secretary is efficient in protecting him from unwelcome callers. On the other hand, heads who make infrequent use of their right of access to the Director may find they receive a sympathetic hearing. This becomes even more likely if they acknowledge the help they have received from people lower in the County Hall hierarchy when there is an outstanding issue on which they need the Director's personal help or guidance. The director is then less likely to feel compelled to defend a colleague, and the colleague is less likely to resent the head's decision to go over his or her head.

The same principles apply within schools. When seeking advice from a colleague senior to one's immediate head of department, it is important: (a) to choose the issue carefully; (b) to ensure that the routine channels for communication have proved inadequate; (c) to avoid, as far as possible, undermining an immediate superior, distinguishing between a point of principle and a disagreement with an individual. Yet although the ability to seek guidance from the school's senior management – using the hierarchy – can be important, it should seldom be necessary if constructive relationships exist with colleagues in less senior positions.

Too often, teachers condone a system which leaves them to learn important parts of the job by trial and error – a notoriously inefficient way of learning. A good example involves meetings with parents to discuss their child's work. Few inexperienced teachers find this easy, especially when they themselves are concerned about the pupil's progress and behaviour. Being present while a senior colleague interviews a parent can be a valuable way of gaining experience, as can joint interviews which can subsequently be discussed with the colleague. Lack of time for such exercises is a legitimate objection, but can be overcome if the will exists. One obvious possibility is for two teachers to be released for 30 minutes during assembly.

The initiative here need not necessarily come from senior staff. Most people in positions of authority like to be asked for their help and advice, and like to think they provide a good model for their colleagues. Newly-appointed members of staff have greater scope than they often believe for taking the initiative in their own professional development. The more they ask senior colleagues for guidance, advice and suggestions, the more they are likely to get. The same applies to older teachers at risk of a burn-out. Probably the best way of preventing burn-out is a sense of developing new and satisfying skills, combined with changing, though not overwhelming responsibilities. The role of the head and senior management team is clearly important, but here, too, the relationship need not be one way. Teachers themselves can take the initiative in preventing the apathy and indifference associated with burn-out. The new INSET arrangements provide opportunities to extend existing interests and to acquire new ones, while the curriculum changes currently taking place offer much greater scope than previously for developing alternative areas of expertise.

Whose responsibility?

An increasingly influential theory of motivation holds that people think of reasons for their success or failure in a task, and that these reasons, or attributions, influence their motivation in future tasks. Weiner (1979) a leading attribution theorist, identified three dimensions on which students attribute their successes or failures. The first consists of causes which are *external or internal* to the individual. The second consists of *stable or unstable* causes depending on whether they refer to a permanent state, for example 'I'm just not bright enough' or a temporary one, for example 'I had 'flu that day'. The third refers to *controllable or uncontrollable* causes, according to the extent to which the subject is able to influence what happens, for example 'I couldn't concentrate because it was too hot', or 'I couldn't concentrate because I couldn't be bothered to change when it got hot'.

Weiner argued that each of these three dimensions is related to motivation. Internal attributions, for example, are associated with self-confidence and high self-esteem when the student is successful and with shame in cases of failure. Whether the feelings of shame increase or reduce subsequent motivation will depend on whether students attribute their failure to stable factors such as the difficulty of the subject, or unstable ones such as their state of health on the day in question. It will also depend on how far students feel able to control what happens to them.

This has some interesting implications both for the way teachers think about the reasons for children's learning and behavioural difficulties, and for the sort of guidance they seek from senior colleagues. Briefly, if we attribute children's problems to external factors over which we have no control and which we cannot realistically expect to change, our own motivation to seek ways of helping them will be drastically reduced. An example is: 'It's always been a problem family; what can you expect?' Conversely, if we acknowledge our own potential influence, emphasising the adaptability of the curriculum and classroom régime, our motivation is likely to be maintained at a higher level. Two examples here are 'Try looking at these materials; they suggest ways that the project could be made more interesting by building on the children's own cultural experience', or 'Many parents have been hostile towards the school in the past; let's look at ways to involve them more actively in what we are trying to do for their children'.

Attribution theory indicates the importance of considering carefully what teachers themselves can do about welfare issues. Teachers, and social workers, can easily become emotionally involved in the domestic problems of some children. If we become submerged in the child's problems we are likely to add to them, not reduce them. The school's role is ably described by Ramsay (1983) in his account of his research in multi-ethnic primary schools serving socially disadvantaged parts of South Auckland, New Zealand. Ramsay demonstrated that the schools varied widely in their effectiveness in terms of pupils' work and behaviour. In the less effective schools teachers tended to attribute the children's learning problems to cultural and family factors. They also tended to make little effort to present the curriculum in ways that built on the pupils' own cultural background. In contrast, teachers in the more effective schools, placed greater emphasis on what *they* could do to motivate the children with an explicit attempt to build on the children's own experiences and cultures.

Conclusions

Working relationships between teachers permeate throughout the school. Children are quick to sense friction and disagreement. Without necessarily being told, they also learn what behaviours different teachers consider acceptable. At the same time, staff relationships inevitably affect the way teachers feel about their work and how they think about the needs of children. A teacher's sense of professional identity depends very largely on his or her membership of a school's staff. Following appointment to a school, a process of socialisation takes place in which the newcomer is encouraged to accept the existing *mores*, written and unwritten. This process is strikingly evident in the case of teachers straight from college or university. At worst, the message can be: 'forget all that theory they taught you on your B. Ed./PGCE; you're at the chalk face now!' At best, as implied in the work of Ramsay (1983) and Mortimore *et al* (1988) the focus is on maintaining a climate which fosters high standards of work and behaviour.

There is far more to this than merely providing supportive relationships between members of staff though these are certainly necessary. Setting high professional standards for children's behaviour and educational progress is challenging and potentially stressful: the higher the standards set, the greater the risk of not achieving them. Children with learning or behavioural problems illustrate this argument.

It is tempting to attribute these problems to the children's genetic endowment and social background. In the short run this reduces stress by providing a ready explanation for the problems which we as teachers are experiencing. In the long run, though, it leads to increased stress since no solution is apparent. Accepting that we play a critical part in children's educational welfare, and may thereby give them the strength and confidence to cope with adverse family circumstances, may increase feelings of stress in the short term but carries the longer term possibility of exploring possible responses with colleagues.

Taking a commitment to the pupils' personal and social welfare seriously leaves teachers open to feelings of frustration and disappointment when the most carefully planned and conscientious efforts prove unsucccessful. Yet we can probably learn more from these incidents than from the less frequent occasions in which everything goes according to plan. However, it takes unusually strong personalities to carry out a rigorous evaluation of their own work unless the underlying ethos accepts unsuccessful efforts as potentially valuable learning experiences, not as an indication of personal or professional inadequacy.

Questions and exercises

1. You have just had a difficult interview with the parent of your most disruptive pupil. The parent has accused you of picking on his/her son, and has stormed out of the school threatening to complain to the office (County Hall). Role play the *post mortem* with the deputy head or head.
2. Can schools avoid a hierarchical structure? Is participatory democracy in schools a realistic possibility?
3. Ask each person in a small group to write one or two paragraphs explaining how, as a newly appointed head of department, or post-holder in a primary school, you should seek to enlist your colleagues' active co-operation. Then use the principal strategies proposed by each person as the basis for discussion.
4. How can the privacy of the classroom be broken down?
5. Do you accept Hargreaves'argument that professional autonomy is a mask for anxieties about being evaluated by colleagues?
6. What impact do *you* think government initiatives since 1980 will have on working relationships between teachers?

7. What survival strategies are available to teachers who find themselves expected by colleagues to attribute children's learning and behavioural difficulties to their genetic endowment and social background?

Recommended reading

Dunham, J. (1984) *Stress in Teaching*. London, Croom Helm.

Edelwich, J. and Brodsky, A. (1980) *Burn-out: Stages of Disillusionment in the Helping Professions*. New York, Human Services Press.

Nias, J. (1980) Leadership Styles and Job Satisfaction in Primary Schools. In Bush, T., Glatter, R. and Riches, C. (Eds.) *Approach to School Management*. London, Harper and Row.

Ramsay, P. (1983) Fresh Perspectives on the School Transformation-Reproduction Debate: A Response to Anyon from the Antipodes. *Curriculum Inquiry*, **13**, 295–320.

CHAPTER 10

Teaching or welfare? Teaching and welfare?

Introduction

This book has argued that pupil welfare is an integral part of every teacher's job, that schools cannot function without affecting their pupils' personal and social development, and that the welfare aspects of teaching require at least some counselling skills. In theory some teachers might achieve excellent academic results from pupils, yet be utterly uninterested in their welfare as individuals. Teachers often claim to have colleagues like this, usually referring to them with disdain or with grudging respect as ex-grammar school people who yearn for the good old days. Yet in practice this argument has 2 flaws.

First, teachers with a strong academic orientation usually *do* take an active interest in the welfare of their academically able pupils, even if they deny an interest in supposedly new-fangled notions like pastoral care or personal and social education. Second, it is hard to provide either an educational or an ethical justification for concentrating on an academically able élite of pupils if the results of the average and below average majority are, at best, mediocre. Interestingly, one of the criticisms levelled at teachers by the political 'new right' is just this: pre-occupation with the needs of an academic élite, at the expense of the majority. Williamson (1980) argued in a different context:

. . . while some children are "guided", "counselled" and "supported" through a successful school career, others (the "less able", the disadvantaged, etc), are "processed" to accept a system in which they are destined to be failures. For want of a better word I shall call this process *pastoralisation*. (p. 172)

In other words, the argument that high educational standards can be achieved without attention to pupils' welfare fails precisely because it is the most able whose welfare needs are most frequently recognised and met.

Of course, these needs may not be met through the bureaucratic and hierarchical systems that sometimes constitute the pastoral network. Nor are they likely to be met in the often ideologically and politically confused activities known as tutorial or personal and social education programmes. These programmes *may* play an important part in pupils' experience at school, but this is only likely if their aims, ethos and methods are consistent with those in the rest of the curriculum. This does not imply the need for any particular style of teaching. The controversy between advocates of 'formal' and 'progressive' methods, for example, is irrelevant because the scope for differences in approach within each style is so great (e.g. Bennett, 1976). Nor, for the same reason, does it imply the need for any particular form of school organisation, for example mixed ability or ability banding (e.g. Gregory, 1984).

On the other hand, a commitment to pupils' welfare and to their personal and social development does have implications for the ethos or social climate which teachers seek to create throughout the school and in their own classrooms. It also has implications for the way they monitor and evaluate their work. Further, the government and many LEAs share with most teachers the view that schools should foster pupils' personal and social development. The problem, of course, is that this means different things to different people.

The government's views, as expressed in DES policy documents, will not be accepted by all LEAs. Within schools teachers will differ both in the priority they attach to different aspects of their welfare-related activities and on how they tackle them. This will depend on their political, cultural and religious values as well as on their own previous training and experience. Yet although they may have conflicting views, the government and LEA policy makers have a legitimate interest in the personal and social education provided in schools, and in how teachers define and cater for their pupils' welfare needs. Head teachers and governors have an equally legitimate interest. How, then, may these potentially incompatible interests be reconciled? Will the resulting tension be creative or destructive?

Government, LEA and teacher interests: a creative tension?

Government

To say that governments should not be concerned about the personal and social education provided in schools would be extraordinary. Almost as a matter of definition, every government has a legitimate, indeed necessary, interest in the personal values and qualities of school leavers as well as in their knowledge and skills. Personal values and qualities will have been influenced by the quality of care they have received throughout their school careers. It follows that the government must be concerned about pupil welfare, using the term in its broadest sense.

In any democracy political parties differ in the priorities they attach to different values, and perhaps also in the values they consider important. The view that the government in a democracy should seek a broad consensus on education is naive. Educational policy making is as much a political process as foreign policy or financial policy. An equally naive view is that once a government has determined the structure of an education system, for example, whether secondary education should be selective, it should sit back and let the professionals take over. That would be like making a decision to run a prison system but allowing judges and magistrates to decide the offences for which people should be sent to them.

A legitimate criticism of Labour Party policy on education in the 1960s and 1970s was that it made just this mistake. It encouraged LEAs to replace grammar and secondary modern schools with comprehensives without any clear ideas as to how the new comprehensives would cater for the needs of the full ability range. As a result, many comprehensives simply reproduced grammar school values, catering well for an academic élite, to the relative neglect of pupils who might have done well in the best secondary moderns, (see, Reynolds *et al*, 1987).

The task of democratic governments is to produce workable policies consistent with their election manifestoes. It is not the task of governments to implement these policies, but rather to ensure that they are capable of being implemented. The distinction is important. Only a totalitarian government could implement its own education policies, since this would require Party membership as a requirement for appointment as teachers, and/or regular classroom inspection by party officials.

The emphasis, then, is on production of *workable* policies. In a democracy these cannot be narrowly party political since their implementation depends on the agreement, or at least acquiescence of employing LEAs and of teachers, both of whom may have an unshakable commitment to the values and priorities of a different party. Education policy as R.A. Butler insisted is the art of the possible, since without the co-operation of teachers, and perhaps also of LEAs it cannot be implemented. What, then, does this imply about the government's role in pupil welfare and personal and social education?

The present government has used a wide range of strategies from legislation to financial inducements to persuade teachers to accept curriculum changes. Besides the national curriculum, these include GCSE and major initiatives on the education of students aged 14–19. In addition, the government has passed legislation which aims to make schools more sensitive to the aspirations of their pupils' parents, and has created two new categories of school: city technical colleges and grant-maintained schools. The explicit hope in each case is that the new schools will promote not only the knowledge and skills the government considers important, but also the attitudes and values.

What the government cannot do as long as we remain a democracy is to dictate how its policies are implemented. It is not inconceivable that the Secretary of State for Education and Science may wake up one morning to discover that he has awarded grant-maintained status to schools with governing bodies controlled by fundamentalist religious sects or fringe political groups such as the National Front or Militant Tendency. Admittedly, he has powers to deal with this kind of situation, but using them would be politically embarrassing.

When it comes to implementation of policy at classroom level the government has even less power. Nowhere is this more evident than in the field of personal and social education. Just as civil servants are able to modify or subvert policies with which they disagree, as the television comedy series *Yes Minister* so effectively demonstrated, so teachers are usually able to subvert policies foisted on them from above. As Secretary of State, Sir Keith Joseph fumed and fulminated over the alleged left-wing bias in some peace studies programmes in secondary schools but succeeded only in giving them additional publicity.

The government clearly cannot legislate for the nature of personal and social education to be provided in schools, if only because pupils' personal and social development is affected by all their experiences at school. Yet it does not follow that a government should express no interest nor claim any involvement in it. A significant achievement of government in the 1980s was to put the social functions of schooling firmly on the political and educational agenda. One may admire or detest its emphasis on competition, enterprise, acquisition of vocationally relevant skills and development of 'responsible' (conformist?) attitudes. Teachers probably differ as much as other members of society in their attitude to these, agreeing only in their dislike of the government's sustained attack on their own professional autonomy. That, however, is not the point. Active agreement *and* active disagreement are potentially fruitful if they lead to evaluation and re-appraisal of a school's aims, policies and practices. The worst that can happen in any educational setting is a complacent belief that 'we think we've got everything just about right now'! The fact that the government appears to have a particular model of the sort of personal and social qualities schools should be developing in their pupils does not mean that teachers need to, or will, accept this model. It does mean that they will need to think hard about their reasons for rejecting it, and that should be a beneficial process.

Local education anthorities

At first sight, LEAs seem to have been emasculated by the 1988 Education Reform Act. Although it is not clear whether they will survive the 1990s in their present form, we should not write them off too quickly. They will certainly retain important responsibilities for monitoring the introduction of the national curriculum and for local inspection of schools. They are likely, too, to retain involvement in INSET. This will be crucial if they are to retain an educational function as opposed to a purely administrative one. In this connection their task will be to interpret centrally-determined policies, and thereby to act as a check on them or, theoretically, to accelerate their introduction. No-one can realistically expect every primary and secondary school in the country to have teachers with sufficient time or expertise to assimilate the flood of curriculum and other directives that will inevitably follow from the 1988 Act, let alone to recognise the variety of ways they may be interpreted. With no guidance from the LEA, implementation will at best be haphazard and ill-prepared, and at worst utterly chaotic.

If this argument is correct, LEAs will need to adopt a much more pro-active role than many of them have taken in the past. It means that they will need to persuade sceptical head teachers and governors that they have valuable services to offer. Teachers will use these services when they recognise and respect not only the expertise of their members, but also that they are sufficiently well staffed and well resourced to be accessible when needed.

LEAs have no more scope than central government for dictating policy and practice on pupil welfare or on personal and social education. They can nevertheless influence what happens in schools in a variety of ways. This starts with a clear articulation of their own policies and values, backed up with programmes for implementing these. Such policies have become more necessary in the light of legislation during the 1980s, not less.

Thus, a lead from the LEA is needed partly as a check on the impact of advice and directives from the DES, and partly to help teachers assimilate and interpret government policies on education. The continuing survival of LEAs may well depend on how effectively teachers see them fulfilling this responsibility. In the final resort, though, it is teachers who determine the nature and quality of welfare and of personal and social education provided in schools.

Schools

This book has argued that schools will affect pupils' personal and social development by the mere fact that pupils attend them. It is precisely because all social organisations such as schools, churches or youth clubs inevitably provide experiences which affect their members' attitudes and values that the responsible adults should be clear about the kind of attitudes and values they are trying to encourage. A 'whole-school' policy on pupil welfare will consider how the school should cater for its less able and/or less conformist members, but will do this in the context of what it is trying to achieve for *all* pupils.

In schools, as with government policy, implementation is the art of the possible. A frequent mistake of newly appointed heads is trying to do too much too quickly and thereby unifying in opposition those key members of staff whose support is essential. High-sounding claims for the school's pastoral care network and for its attention to the personal and social development of each individual can be found in many school prospectuses. We have argued that these have both organisational and curriculum implications. There is no point in expecting form tutors to carry out pastoral duties if they only see their tutees for registration purposes. There is no point in talking about a personal and social education programme unless teachers see how their own teaching can contribute to this. More important, though, school policy on welfare should both develop and reflect the ethos, or moral climate of the school as a whole. The policy should reflect the school's ethos in the sense that it is based on what colleagues and pupils recognise and respect as good practice, and extend it in the sense that further progress and development are seen as possible.

This implies not only that teachers have a sense of responsibility for their pupils' personal, social and educational welfare, but also that they are prepared to carry out a rigorous evaluation of their own work. There is an interesting parallel between teachers' and pupils' coping strategies when faced with potentially stressful demands. Many less successful pupils, including those defined as having special educational needs are regarded by teachers as disruptive, are reluctant to seek help when unable to complete a task and tend to adopt one of two equally negative strategies. The first is to attribute their learning problem to lack of ability, with the implication that this is something they can do nothing about. The second is to attribute their learning problem to lack of interest: 'It's not that I can't do it; it's just that I don't care. It's boring!' The first strategy has been described as 'learned helplessness', while the second may be seen as an attempt to maintain a sense of self-worth (see Craske, 1988).

As Hargreaves (1982) has eloquently argued, many schools are unsupportive places for the adults who work in them. Teachers can find themselves adopting similar strategies to their pupils. Teachers who feel there is nothing much they can do about their pupils' behaviour or progress because 'it's a bad area' or 'he/she comes from a problem family; they've been known to all the agencies for years', are exhibiting a 'learned helpless' response. Teachers who insist to anyone who will listen that they are teachers not social workers, and if a child doesn't want to learn, well, that's just too bad, are exhibiting the self-worth maintenance strategy.

Each strategy is a way of avoiding evaluation, and the short-term benefits should be recognised. To evaluate their own work leaves people open to criticism from colleagues. It requires honest but supportive relationships between members of staff. It does not involve prolonged involvement in esoteric activities conducted by outside experts, but rather a continuing process of discussion and negotiation between colleagues.

Talking about an unpleasant incident involving a protection racket, a deputy head arranged to meet the teachers who had dealt with it. The questions he put to them appeared at first sight very simple: What led up to the incident? How did we as a school deal with it? What do we think the offenders will have learned? What may their victims and the other pupils have learned? Was this what we intended? What have *we* learned from this incident? What might we have done differently? The questions were simple, but the answers were not. They raised the not unimportant possibility that the severity of the punishment given to the pupils concerned might have had the unintended consequence of increasing their victims' anxiety and their sense of isolation in the school. They also raised questions about lunch hour supervision, about ways of dealing with a small but tightly-knit group of fourth year pupils who were priding themselves on rejection of the school's values and about ways of creating a climate in which similar incidents in the future would come to teachers' attention at an earlier stage.

The evaluation of this incident, then, raised short, medium and long-term questions. In the short-term the welfare of the pupils who had suffered from the protection racket needed to be considered. In the medium term there was the question of lunch-hour supervision. In the long-term the incident had confirmed the existence of fundamental problems in social relationships in the school. These could not be dealt with quickly, nor, in the deputy's view, would introducing a programme of personal and social education be even remotely relevant. He agreed with the probationer teacher who had said at the meeting: 'They all know they will only be entered for one or two GCSEs, and probably won't get them. They think we've written them off as failures, what's more, they're right and they're getting their own back'.

The protection racket involved incidents outside the classroom, but the same principles apply to evaluation of counselling interviews and of classroom activities. Evaluation starts with questions like: Did the children do what I intended? What did they learn? What did *I* learn? What might I have done differently? What do I do next? Self-evaluation is a necessary starting point, but evaluation is usually much more useful when carried out with colleagues. This helps us to see how others see us, not just how we see ourselves. It does, however, require that we find time to observe colleagues teaching and that we ourselves expect to be observed. The same applies to interviews with parents.

This brings us back to the importance of open and supportive relationships between colleagues. It is these relationships which produce a climate which encourages the kind of on-going evaluation we have been describing. A school's impact on its pupils' personal and social development is determined not by what happens in a PSE programme but by the totality of their learning experience in the school. In other words the critical factor is the school's overall ethos. In the same way, the usefulness of evaluation is not determined by a few necessarily artificial exercises on INSET days to review specific developments. Rather, it is determined by the prevailing ethos amongst the staff, whether they make a habit of reviewing their work, discussing alternative approaches, looking constructively for more effective ways to work with particular pupils or classes. The underlying climate can inhibit evaluation, or make it a habit that teachers take for granted as a necessary and desirable part of the job.

Conclusions

Evaluation can be stressful. It can also enhance job satisfaction, partly by providing opportunities for teachers' professional development and partly by indicating ways to improve the quality of children's learning at school. This applies as much to welfare and counselling activities as to the curriculum. Yet attention to pupils' welfare is unlikely to be effective unless teachers also think of their own and their colleagues' welfare. The schools which provide the highest quality of personal and social education for their pupils tend to be those in which high job-satisfaction amongst the teachers is based on continuing professional growth and development.

Continuing professional growth and development implies a sense of direction, which in turn implies that schools articulate the kind of educational and social climate they are seeking to create. This will not be found in the pages of a curriculum development or PSE programme. It certainly will not be produced by DES diktat, let alone by an act of parliament. It will be produced at school level by teachers who are responsive to the needs of their pupils and the aspirations of the communities they serve. It will recognise that the educational and the social functions of schools are inextricably interlinked, seeing pupils' personal and social development as a responsibility of all teachers throughout the curriculum. It will also be sensitive to the needs of less able and/or less cooperative pupils, recognising that the morality of a school, as of a legal system, is judged at least in part by how it treats its least privileged or least conformist members. In demanding high standards of work from all pupils it will ensure that the attainments of the academically least able pupils are valued as highly as those of the most able. In demanding high standards of behaviour it will encourage expression of individual interests while fostering a socially responsible acceptance among pupils of their rights and responsibilities within the school and outside it. Such schools exist. They are challenging, but exciting and satisfying places both for pupils and for teachers. I hope this book will provoke discussion that helps more teachers to achieve this kind of climate.

Questions and exercises

1. Discuss Williamson's argument that only successful pupils are 'guided', 'counselled' and 'supported', with reference to your present school. Is it fair to say that the less able are '*processed* to accept a system in which they are destined to be failures'?
2. Write an alternative prospectus entry on the school's personal and social education programme from the point of view of your most difficult pupil. How much truth is there in what the 'pupil' writes?
3. Debate the motion that 'The Conservative government of the 1980s succeeded in putting personal and social education on the political and educational agenda.'
4. Working in groups, prepare a 1–2 page policy statement on pupil welfare for your LEA.
5. Discuss the 'learned helplessness' and 'self-worth maintenance' strategies described in the text with reference to pupils in a class you know well. Do you see any parallel in your own responses to difficult situations?

Recommended reading

Clemett, A. J. and Pearce, J. S. (1986) *The Evaluation of Pastoral Care.* Oxford, Blackwell.
Williamson, D. (1980) 'Pastoral Care' or 'Pastoralization'? In Best, R., Jarvis, C. and Ribbins, P. (Eds.) *Perspectives on Pastoral Care.* Oxford, Blackwell.

REFERENCES

Baldwin, J. and Wells, H. (1979) *Active Tutorial Work. Book 1, The First Year – Book 5, The Fifth Year*, Oxford, Blackwell

Bennett, N. (1976) *Teaching Styles and Pupil Progress*, London, Open Books

Bennett, N. (1980) *Open Plan Schools: Teaching, Curriculum, Design*, Windsor, NFER

Bennet, N., Desforges, C., Cockburn, A., and Wilkinson, B. (1984) *The Quality of Pupil Learning Experiences*, London, Lawrence Erlbaum

Berger, M. (1982) 'Applied behaviour analysis in education: A critical assessment and some implications for training teachers'. *Educational Psychology*, **2**, p. 289–300.

Best, R., Jarvis, C. and Ribbins, P. (Eds) (1980) *Perspectives on Pastoral Care*, London, Heinemann

Best, R., Ribbins, P., Jarvis, C. with Oddy, D. (1983) *Education and Care*, London, Heinemann

Blatt, M. and Kohlberg, L. (1973) 'The effects of classroom moral discussion on children's level of moral judgement', in L. Kohlberg (Ed) *Collected Papers on Moral Development and Moral Judgement*, Harvard University, Moral Education and Research Foundation

Bowles, S. and Gintis, H. (1976) *Schooling in Capitalist America*, London, Routledge and Kegan Paul

Brennan, W. (1987) 'Once more into the core', *Special Children*, **XIV** (October), 14–15.

Burton, L. (Ed) (1974) *The Care of the Child Facing Death*, London, Routledge and Kegan Paul

Button, L. (1981) *Group Tutoring for the Form Teacher: A Developmental Model*, Book 1: Lower Secondary School, Book 2: Upper Secondary School, London, Hodder and Stoughton

Coates, T. J. and Thoresen, C. E. (1976) 'Teacher Anxiety: A review with recommendations', *Review of Educational Research*, **46**, p. 159–184.

Coleman, J. B. *et al* (1966) *Equality of Educational Opportunity*, Washington, US Government Printing Office

Coopers and Lybrand (1988) *Local Management of Schools: A Report to the Department of Education and Science*, London, DES

Cox, C. B. and Boyson, R. (1977) *Black Paper 1977*, London, Maurice Temple Smith

Cox, K. and Lavelle, M. (1982) *Staff Development Through Teacher Interaction: A School-based Case Study*, Sheffield, Sheffield City Polytechnic, Department of Educational Management

Craske, M. L. (1988) 'Learned helplessness, self-worth motivation and attribution re-training for primary school children', *British Journal of Educational Psychology*, **58**, p. 152–164

David, K. and Charlton, T. (Eds) (1987) *The Caring Role of the Primary School*, London, Macmillan

Delamont, S. and Galton, M. (1986) *Inside the Secondary Classroom*, London, Routledge and Kegan Paul

Department of Education and Science (1967) *Children and their Primary Schools* (*The Plowden Report*), London, HMSO

Department of Education and Science (1976) *A Language for Life* (*The Bullock Report*), London, HMSO

Department of Education and Science (1978) *Special Educational Needs* (*The Warnock Report*), London, HMSO

Department of Education and Science (1985a) *Better Schools*, London, HMSO

Department of Education and Science (1985b) *Draft Circular: School Attendance and Education Welfare Services*, London, DES

Department of Education and Science (1987a) *AIDS: Some Questions and Answers*, London, DES

Department of Education and Science (1987b) *Sex Education at School*, (*Circular 11/87*), London, DES

Department of Education and Science (1988a) *School Teachers' Pay and Conditions Document, 1988*, London, HMSO

Department of Education and Science (1988b) *National Curriculum: Task Groups on Assessment*, London, DES

Department of Education and Science (1988c) *Working Together for the Protection of Children from Abuse: Procedures within the Education Service*, London, DES

Department of Education and Science / Her Majesty's Inspectors of Schools (1977), *Curriculum 11–16*, London, DES

Department of Education and Science / Her Majesty's Inspectors of Schools (1980) *A View of the Curriculum*, London, HMSO

Department of Health and Social Security (1968) *Report of the Committee on Local Authority and Allied Personal Social Services* (*The Seebohm Report*), London, HMSO

Department of Health and Social Security (1974) *Report of the Committee of Inquiry into the Care and Supervision Provided in Relation to Maria Colwell*, London, HMSO

Department of Health and Social Security (1988) *Working Together for the Protection of Children from Abuse* (*Circular 26/88*), London, DHSS

Dweck, C., Davidson, W., Nelson, S. and Bradley, E. (1978) 'Sex differences in learned helplessness', 'II contingencies of evaluative feedback in the classroom', 'III An experimental analysis', *Development Psychology*, **14**, p. 268–276

Dyer, H. S. (1968) 'School factors and equal educational opportunity', *Harvard Educational Review*, **38**, p. 38–56

Edelwich, J. and Brodsky, A. (1980) *Burn-Out: Stages of Disillusionment in the Helping Professions*, New York, Human Services Press

Egglestone, J., Dunn, D. and Anjali, M. (1986) Education for some: Educational and Vocational Experiences of 15–18 year old members of minority ethnic groups, (with ethnographic study by C. Wright). London: Trewham Books.

Fitzherbert, K. (1977) *Child Care Services and the Teacher*, London, Maurice Temple Smith

French, J. and French, P. (1984) 'Gender imbalances in the primary classroom: an interactional account', *Educational Research* 26, p. 127–136

Galloway, D. (1976) *Case Studies in Classroom Management*, London, Longman

Galloway, D. (1983) 'Disruptive pupils and effective pastoral care', *School Organisation*, 3, p. 245–254

Galloway, D. (1985) *Schools and Persistent Absentees*, Oxford, Pergamon

Galloway, D. (1987) 'Teachers, Parents and Other Professionals', in K. David and T. Charlton (Eds), *The Caring Role of the Primary School*, London, Macmillan

Galloway, D., Ball, T., Blomfield, D. and Seyd, R. (1982) *Schools and Disruptive Pupils*, London, Longman

Galloway, D., Boswell, K., Panckhurst, F., Boswell, C. and Green, K. (1985) 'Sources of satisfaction and dissatisfaction for New Zealand primary school teachers', *Educational Research*, 27, p. 44–51

Galloway, D. and Goodwin, C. (1987) *The Education of Disturbing Children: Pupils with Learning and Adjustment Difficulties*, London, Longman

Galloway, D., Mortimore, P. and Tutt, N. (1989) 'Enquiry into Discipline in Schools: Evidence from the Departments of Educational Research and Social Administration, University of Lancaster', in N. Jones (Ed) *Schoo' Curriculum and Pupil Behaviour*, Lewes: Falmer

Galloway, D., Panckhurst, F., Boswell, K., Boswell, C. and Green, K. (1987) 'Sources of stress for class teachers in New Zealand primary schools', *Pastoral Care in Education*, 5, p. 28–36.

Garlick, R. (1976) *Poems 1972–1975*, Gwasg, Gower

Gillham, B. (Ed) (1978) *Reconstructing Educational Psychology*, London, Croom Helm

Goacher, B., Evans, J., Welton, J. and Wedell, K. (1988) *Policy and Provision for Special Educational Needs: Implementing the 1981 Education Act*, London: Cassell

Goldacre, P. (1978) 'Work with bereaved boys in a secondary school', *Theraupeutic Education*, 6, ii, p. 26–27

Gray, J. and Hannon, V. (1986) 'Interpretations of schools' examination results', *Journal of Educational Policy*, 1, p. 23–33

Gregory, R. P. (1984) 'Streaming, setting and mixed ability grouping in primary and secondary schools: some research findings', *Educational Studies*, 10, p. 209–226

Hargreaves, D. H. (1982) *The Challenge for the Comprehensive School: Culture, Curriculum and Community*, London, Routledge and Kegan Paul

Her Majesty's Inspector of Schools (1984) *The Educational Welfare Service: An Enquiry into Eight LEAs*, London, DES

Hewison, J. and Tizard, J. (1980) 'Parental involvement and reading attainment', *British Journal of Educational Psychology*, 50, p. 209–215

Holdaway, E. A. (1978) 'Facet and overall satisfaction of teachers', *Educational Administrative Quarterly*, **14**, p. 30–47

Johnson, D. and Ransom, E. (1983) *Family and School*, London, Croom Helm

Jones, A. (1984) *Counselling Adolescents: School and After*, London, Kogan Page

Kelly, A., Whyte, J. and Smail, B. (1984) *Girls into Science and Technology: Final Report*, Manchester, University of Manchester

Kohlberg, L. (1975) *The cognitive developmental approach to moral education, Phi Delta Kappa* **56**, p. 670–677

Lang, P. (Ed) (1988) *Thinking about Personal and Social Education in the Primary School*, Oxford, Blackwell

Lansdown, R. (1980) *More than Sympathy*, London, Tavistock

Levitt, E. E. (1963) 'Psychotherapy with children: A further evaluation', *Behaviour Research and Therapy*, **1**, p. 45–51

Liberman, R. P., King, L. W., De Risi, W. and McCann, M. (1975) 'Personal Effectiveness', *Champaign*, Ill, Research Press

Local Government Training Board (1972) *The Role and Training of Education Welfare Officers: Report of the Working Party*, Luton: Local Government Training Board

London Borough of Brent (1985) *A Child in Trust. The Report of the Panel of Inquiry into the Circumstances Surrounding the Death of Jasmine Beckford*, London, Borough of Brent

London Borough of Greenwich (1987) *A Child in Mind. The Report of the Commission of Inquiry into the Circumstances Surrounding the Death of Kimberley Carlisle*, London, Borough of Greenwich

Macbeth, A. (1984) *The Child Between. A Report on School-Family Relations in the Countries of the European Community*, EEC

McGurk, H. (Ed) (1987) *What Next?* London, Economic and Social Research Council

Macmillan, K. (1980) 'The Education Welfare Officer, past, present and future', in M. Craft, J. Raynor and L. Cohen (Eds) *Linking home and school: A New Review (3rd Edition)*, London, Harper and Row

Manthorpe, C. A. (1980) 'Men's science, women's science or science? Some issues related to the study of girls' science education', *Studies in Science Education*, **9**, p. 65–80

Marland, M. (1975) *The Craft of the Classroom: A Survival Guide*, London, Heinemann

Marland, M. (Ed) (1983) *Sex Differentiation and Schooling*, London: Heinemann

Marland, M. (1985) 'Parents, Schooling and the Welfare of Pupils', in P. Ribbins (Ed) *Schooling and Welfare*, Lewes, Falmer

Maslow, A. H. (1970) *Motivation and Personality (2nd Edition)*, NY, Harper and Row

Mille, R. (1987) 'English schools and pastoral care as perceived by French teachers', *Pastoral care in Education*, **5**, p. 9–15

Mitchell, S. and Rosa, P. (1981) Boyhood behaviour problems as precursors of criminality: A fifteen year follow-up. *Journal of Child Psychology and Psychiatry*, **22**, p. 19–33

Mortimore, P., Sammons, P., Stoll, L., Lewis, D. and Ecob, R.

(1988) *School Matters: The Junior Years*, Wells, Open Books

Munro, E. A., Manthei, R. J. and Small, J. J. (1979) *Counselling: A Skills Approach*, Wellington, N.Z., Methuen

Neill, A. S. (1937) *That Dreadful School*, London, H. Jenkins

Newbold, D. D. (1977) *Ability Grouping – The Banbury Inquiry*, Windsor, NFER

New Zealand Department of Education (1977) *Growing, Sharing, Learning – The Report of the Committee on Health and Social Education (The Johnson Report)*, Wellington, N.Z., Government Printer

Nias, J. (1980), 'Leadership styles and job satisfaction in Primary Schools', in T. Bush, R. Glatter and C. Riches (Eds) *Approach to School Management*, London, Harper and Row

Nisbet, J. and Schucksmith, J. (1986) *Learning Strategies*, London, Routledge

Peter, M. (1986) 'Picking up the bill for disruption', *Times Educational Supplement*, 22 April, p. 4

Pratt J. (1978) Perceived stress among teachers: the effects of age and background of children taught. *Educational Review*, **30**, 3–14

Pratt, J. D. (1983) 'Law and social control: A study of truancy and school deviancy', *British Journal of Law and Society*, **10**, p. 223–240

Ramsay, P. (1983) 'Fresh perspectives on the school transformation reproduction debate: A response to Anyon from the Antipodes', *Curriculum Inquiry*, **13**, p. 295–320

Reynolds, D. (1976) 'When teachers and pupils refuse a truce: The secondary school and the creation of delinquency', in G. Mungham and G. Pearson (Eds) *Working Class Youth Culture*, London, Routledge and Kegan Paul

Reynolds, D., Sullivan, M. and Murgatroyd, S. (1987) *The Comprehensive Experiment: A comparison of the Selective and Non-Selective System of School Organisation*, Lewes, Falmer

Riseborough, G. F. (1985) 'Pupils, teachers' careers and schooling: an empirical study', in S. J. Ball and I. F. Goodson (Eds) *Teachers' Lives and Careers*, Lewes, Falmer

Roberts, T. (1979) 'The hidden curriculum in the infants school', *Durham and Newcastle Research Review*, **8**, 42, p. 29–33

Robins, L. N. (1972) 'Follow-up studies of behaviour disorder in children', in H. C. Quay and J. S. Werry, *Psychopathological Disorders of Childhood*, New York, Wiley

Rutter, M. (1978) 'Family, area and school influences in the genesis of conduct disorders', in L. Hersov, M. Berger and D. Schaffer (Eds) *Aggression and Anti-social Behaviour in Childhood and Adolescence*, Oxford, Pergamon

Rutter, M. (1981) 'Stress, coping and development: some issues and some questions', *Journal of Child Psychology and Psychiatry*, **22**, p. 323–356

Rutter, M., Tizard, J. and Whitmore, K. (1970) *Education, Health and Behaviour*, London, Longman

Rutter, M., Maughan, B., Mortimore, P. and Ouston, J. (1979) *Fifteen Thousand Hours: Secondary Schools and their Effects on Pupils* London, Open Books

Sergiovanni, T. (1967) 'Factors which affect satisfaction and dissatisfaction of teachers', *Journal of Educational Administration*, **5**, p. 66–82

Stone, M. (1981) *The Education of the Black child in Britain*, London, Fontana

Surkes, S. (1988) 'In dispute over whether to help parent or pupils. What the letter from Number 10 said', *Times Educational Supplement*, p. 18, March 6

Sutherland, M. (1981) *Sex Bias in Education*, Oxford, Blackwell

Tizard, B. and Hughes, M. (1984) *Young Children Learning*, London, Fontana

Tizard, J. (1973) 'Maladjusted children and the child guidance service', *London Educational Review*, **2**, p. 22–37

Tizard, J., Schofield, W. N. and Hewison, J. (1982) 'Collaboration between teachers and parents in assisting children's reading', *British Journal of Educational Psychology*, **52**, p. 1–15

Tomlinson, S. (1982) *The Sociology of Special Education*, London, Routledge and Kegan Paul

Vogelaar, L. M. E. and Silverman, M. S. (1984) 'Non-verbal communication in cross-cultural counselling: A literature review', *International Journal for the Advancement of Counselling*, **7**, p. 41–57

Warnock, M. (1985) 'Teacher Teach Thyself: The 1985 Richard Dimbleby Lecture', *The Listener*, 28 March, p. 10–14

Weiner, B. (1979) 'A theory of motivation for some classroom experiences', *Journal of Educational Psychology*, **71**, p. 3–25

Whyte, J. (1983) *Beyond the Wendy House: Sex Role Stereotyping in Primary Schools*, London, Schools Council

Whyte, J., Deem, R., Kant, L. and Cruikshank, M. (Eds) (1985) *Girl Friendly Schooling*, London, Methuen

Widlake, P. and MacLoed, F. (1984) *Raising Standards: Parental Involvement Programmes and the Language Performance of Children*, Coventry: Community Education Development Centre

Williamson, D. (1980) '"Pastoral Care" or "Pastoralization"?', in R. Best, C. Jarvis and P. Ribbins (Eds) *Perspectives on Pastoral Care*, London, Heinemann

Young, P. and Tyre, C. (1983) *Dyslexia or Illiteracy? Realising the Right to Read*, Milton Keynes, Open University Press

INDEX

Caerleon
Library